Rx for the Common Core

Rx for the Common Core

Toolkit for Implementing Inquiry Learning

Mary Boyd Ratzer and Paige Jaeger

LIBRARIES UNLIMITED

AN IMPRINT OF ABC-CLIO, LLC

Santa Barbara, California • Denver, Colorado • Oxford, England

Copyright 2014 by Mary Boyd Ratzer and Paige Jaeger

Library of Congress Cataloging-in-Publication Data

Ratzer, Mary Boyd.
  Rx for the common core : toolkit for implementing inquiry learning / Mary Boyd Ratzer
and Paige Jaeger.
    pages cm
    Includes index.
    ISBN 978-1-61069-545-9 (paperback) — ISBN 978-1-61069-546-6 (ebook)   1. Inquiry-based
learning—United States.   2. Education—Standards—United States.   I. Jaeger, Paige.   II. Title.
    LB1027.23.R38 2014
    371.39—dc23   2013041484

ISBN: 978-1-61069-545-9
EISBN: 978-1-61069-546-6

18 17 16 15 14   1 2 3 4 5

This book is also available on the World Wide Web as an eBook.
Visit www.abc-clio.com for details.

Libraries Unlimited
An Imprint of ABC-CLIO, LLC

ABC-CLIO, LLC
130 Cremona Drive, P.O. Box 1911
Santa Barbara, California 93116-1911

This book is printed on acid-free paper ∞

Manufactured in the United States of America

Prologue: Rx for the Common Core

Two pervasive metaphors weave meaning through this book and they are mutually reinforcing: fitness and the fairytale hope of spinning straw into gold. Throughout the book we look at the Common Core State Standards (CCSS) and Inquiry through these two lenses. As the title suggests, the Common Core demands pedagogical fitness, mental weight lifting, more challenging assessment workouts, and deep comprehension of complex text. *Rx for the Common Core* gets to the heart of the matter, conveying the notion that strategic action is the antidote for failing instructional practices.

The second metaphoric lens is an obvious contrast. Harking back to the fairytale of *Rumpelstiltskin,* the notion of spinning straw into gold has pedagogical meaning on a few levels. The learner who is merely fetching facts, dutifully completing rote learning activities, is working with straw. The pedagogical shifts that turn straw into gold are the premise of this book. Inquiry-based learning generates a golden outcome: an engaged, motivated learner who uses, manipulates, applies, contrasts, and synthesizes information to create deep understanding. College and career readiness is golden.

Contents

Introduction

WHAT IS THE PURPOSE OF THIS BOOK?

John Dewey was right. Experience is the best teacher. This practical guide to achieving the goals of the Common Core Learning Standards was written after six years of innovative curriculum design, embedded coaching, and face-to-face engagement with thousands of teachers that proved to be a crucible for exploring and discovering what works for today's millennial learners: Inquiry-Based Learning. These are the foundations of this book.

Change occurs for teachers when they simply realize that old-fashioned stand-and-deliver teaching no longer works. Second graders are "glassy eyed." Content reduced to flash cards is soon forgotten. Grade seven social studies students bring no prior knowledge of the Civil War even though "it was covered" in grade 5. Mile-wide, inch-deep coverage does not foster long-term memory in a circle of passive kids. Scoop-and-spit research facts evaporate when words are transferred from sources to "packets." Big ideas never take shape as science lessons deflate into steps to be followed. Meaning is not constructed. Multiple quality resources are not synthesized. Original conclusions are not made or shared. Questions are frozen as who, what, where, and when. These lessons never answer the How? Or Why? Or Should?

This book provides answers to many pedagogical essential questions. These questions and essential questions (EQ) are enumerated in the TABLE of CONTENTS and serve as the framework for this book on instructional change. The research that illuminates this practice is not new. As the Common Core pulls practice to higher standards for better outcomes, it also converges with the evidence regarding *how* kids learn. The purpose of this book is to demonstrate what successful learning looks like in action.

Inquiry starts with wonder, questioning, brainstorming, and background building. Inquiry progresses to meaningful focus, intense investigation, and experimentation by the learner. Synthesis manifests itself in shared knowledge products, arguments supported by evidence, and deeply analyzed texts. The roadmap to genuine synthesis takes shape in the graphical resources and text in this work. That roadmap takes the educator to backward design, questioning, engagement, and long-term formative knowledge.

These are the engines for college and career readiness. Many proven tools have been included. Teachers can adopt and adapt strategies, charts, and graphical resources. Three fully developed and field-tested resources are included:

- The **Inquiry-Based Curriculum: Library and Information Skills for 21st-Century Learners**—a K–12 matrix of skills, organized by the six steps in an Inquiry process: CONNECT and FOCUS, INVESTIGATE, CONSTRUCT, CREATE, EXPRESS, REFLECT. This had its roots in New York City's Inquiry-based Information Fluency Continuum, which is still viable as the Common Core becomes more prominent. *The Inquiry-Based Curriculum* is fully context dependent and includes performance indicators for literacy, as well as social and ethical responsibilities.

- The WISE *Inquiry Model Teacher's Guide* emerges as a counterpart for an elementary audience, using four Inquiry steps: WONDER, INVESTIGATE, SYNTHESIZE, EXPRESS = **WISE.** Along with performance indicators, WISE includes teacher tools, assessment ideas, a snippet of key research, a brief guide to **essential questions,** knowledge products, backward design, and self-assessment for an Inquiry driven plan. Many secondary teachers have also embraced this model as it is easier to digest and adopt.

- *The WISE Guide to Questioning, Synthesis, and Assessment* drills down to analyze and package the complex and powerful heart of the matter for those who implement Inquiry. This will help teachers become proficient in Inquiry-based learning and the Common Core.

The tools included in this book provide a starting point for educators who want to change, but still need to learn *how* to do that. Use the guidance here to build Common Core learning experiences ignited by Inquiry.

1

Inquiry Basics

INQUIRY, NEW PRACTICE, AND OUTCOMES

The stakes could not be higher right now as educators search for what works and what does not. These questions have sparked a national conversation about learning and teaching. The business community has spoken: How prepared are the graduates of America's schools for 21st-century jobs? Higher education has spoken: How prepared are the graduates of America's schools for the challenges of higher education? Government leaders have spoken: How can America compete when the world is flat, and America's schools graduate about 70% of their kids? Learners have spoken: Why should I stay in school? Why should I care? What does this mean for me? Those who propose change need to listen as well as speak.

Let's Turn to Research and Evidence

Inquiry-based learning (IBL) and the Common Core Learning Standards share a broad and solid research base. Brain-based research and studies out of Stanford support Inquiry-based and collaborative learning. Successful change in Chicago involving authentic intellectual work by students, and the Ontario Study look closely at high-risk learners and the benefit of challenging real-world research tasks and self-assessment.

IBL inherently demands balanced, ongoing assessment that improves student performance. The awakening of curiosity, wonder, and purpose in learners transforms their investment into quality work. In an Inquiry model teachers frequently elicit evidence of student skills and understanding, and coach learners to improve performance at point of need.

Let's Clarify the Important Big Ideas

IBL research consistently highlights the importance of the following pedagogical strategies:

- Engaging the learner through relevance
- Questioning

- Synthesizing facts into meaning
- Writing from sources
- Building knowledge in the content areas using formative and summative assessment
- Emphasizing an authentic knowledge product
- Sharing knowledge products using technology

Let's Consider the Pay Off for Improved Professional Practice

Teachers who master and implement IBL in their classrooms have greater success in transitioning to the Common Core. The intangible rewards of renewed passion, job satisfaction, even fun or excitement color their experiences. When teachers interact with learners about content, rich texts, and real-world connections, meaning and ownership are transferred to the student.

Teacher and student share common learning goals. They can experience mutual success when knowledge products are shared providing evidence of deep understanding and original ideas.

Student learning outcomes can stretch to the *stuff that dreams are made of,* and that is not hyperbole. An inner-city school in upstate New York shifted to an Inquiry model for grade 9, retaining an estimated 150 students that would have otherwise dropped out. Special educators testify to the change in their students in an Inquiry learning environment. Kids who do not work, work. Kids who do not contribute, engage. Kids who are discouraged by pen and paper tasks, tap their talents and excel when they share their investigation creatively. *Wonder* comes back into the lives of science students when Inquiry takes them beyond the "kit" with its prescribed tasks. Voices of motivated high school students reach out beyond the school to their communities and their world. Learners become the independent, resilient, curious, and effective agents of their own success.

Let's Draw the Line in the Sand

The following chart contrasts the problem of disengaged learners to the promise of better outcomes. Consider these real-world scenarios:

Reality check—real-world quotes from the mouth of educators	Scenario subscript	With an Inquiry focus this could look like
"So the kids were doing Blah, Blah, Blah Power Points."	Facts transferred from source to slide, no depth, relevance, context, understanding	Build background, questions, focused investigation, and conclusions based on evidence
"But we already did the holocaust in 8th grade." "All day long I scream history."	Content coverage resulted in a learner familiar with flat content, yet not compelled by it. Text is shallowly considered	Deep reading of compelling texts, develop questions for investigation from multiple perspectives, synthesize a new, empathetic understanding and communicate knowledge
"I know we taught the Civil War in grade 5. In grade 7 kids say— 'What war?'"	Long-term formative knowledge did not occur. Reading, listening, rote recall was short term. No connections to historical conceptual learning	Engage learners with close reading/viewing of primary documents, build background with themes, concepts, voices of witnesses, unify with a central question, launch learners with a focus question and multiple sources, share viewpoints in authentic narratives
"Only 42% of the kids completed the research assignment."	Disconnect with a teacher-directed task, bureaucratic approach to box checking in "packets," disengaged, reading/writing for the grade, no relevance or ownership	A student-centered process: * models expectations while developing skills for a purpose * has student-generated questions, * fosters interrogation of relevant issues * has action-driven outcomes and goals * gathers new understanding used to persuade with evidence
"I made it easier and easier, and they still don't learn." "I can't take the time to go deep."	Reducing content to discreet and linear pieces for short-term recall and selected response testing, does not result in long-term assimilation of content	Big unifying ideas, concepts, and themes that are expressed as essential questions: * drive deep reading * connect related facts into main ideas * foster logical expression of important concepts in writing or speaking * transfers knowledge to new learning

(Continued)

Reality check— real-world quotes from the mouth of educators	Scenario subscript	With an Inquiry focus this could look like
"The one who is doing the work is doing the learning."	Delivering content to passive learners results in limited retention Teacher talk, teacher questioning, teacher-centered activity has limited effectiveness	Active learners read and analyze, listen, share, discuss, question, hypothesize, collaborate, communicate, represent, share, present, review, recall, and connect

EQ: Why Should I Care about How I Package My Delivery?

A captivating story from childhood portrays a princess forced to spin straw into gold. The prospect of this magical transformation is wondrous. No less wondrous is the prospect of today's learner questioning, thinking, synthesizing, and communicating, in effect turning the raw material of facts into the precious and lasting treasure of deep understanding. With the transforming power of IBL and the Common Core Standards, teachers are able to engage their students in an information-to-knowledge journey.

This time of new possibilities, inevitably involves straw and gold. Teachers express frustration and need to emerge from a climate of learning that is characterized by testing, short-term recall of often unrelated facts, rapidly and thinly covered content, and ever-increasing challenges. How can educators engender critical engagement, rigor, relevance, authentic process, depth, and golden outcomes? This can happen through IBL:

- A middle school math teacher mulls over her Common Core expectations for mathematics, readily picking out the golden units that energizes learners, connects them with mathematical thinking, and mathematics as a basis for real-world decisions.

- A third grade teacher is conflicted when weighing her science basal and pacing guide with the promise of genuine wonder, curiosity, student-centered investigations, and shared creative products.

- A high school social studies teacher considers the investment in deep research questions generated by groups planning to impeach Abraham Lincoln, while negotiating his relentless course dictated timetable.

For those educators who seek meaningful investigations, knowledge that sticks, and intellectual curiosity, strategies are in this book. Spinning cognitive straw into gold begins not with *Rumpelstiltskin,* but with Inquiry. Cooperative learning projects transform a bureaucratic educational task into an important conversation. Questioning moves beyond the facts to sift the nuggets out of the silt. Synthesis of information creates big ideas via critical thinking and original conclusions. Inquiry learning ignites the Common Core spinning straw into gold.

If teachers do not care about igniting passion in learning, they will lose the battle for college and career readiness (CCR).

Time to Focus

The Common Core shifts are represented here in a simple graphic to be used as a personal assessment. Can you wrap your head around these pieces with ample understanding and build upon them? Do you know the roles that these shifts and concepts play in creating lessons that are aligned with the Common Core State Standards (CCSS)? Take note of those concepts which are essential understandings.

EQ: Am I Ready? Do I Have the Capacity for Inquiry?

In literally thousands of encounters with administrators, teachers, and school librarians across New York, Inquiry seeds were sown. Some seeds fell on hard ground and did not flourish. Some, like the parable, fell by the wayside; some started to grow but did not have sustaining care. However, many, many, many seeds of Inquiry fell on fertile ground, grew, flourished, spread their roots, and transformed curriculum. A school's culture, existing practice, morale, and vision contribute to Inquiry success. The following attributes are present in a school "ready" for Inquiry:

- A supportive administrator who recognizes the value of IBL
- Time to engage in coaching to develop an Inquiry unit plan during the school day
- Willingness to let go of a teacher-directed approach
- Follow-up for those who need support after an intensive, small group session
- Mutual support of peers, grade level or departmental colleagues, special education experts, subject area experts
- Educators who exhibit risk taking and openness to new ideas
- Clear goals for transforming practice sustained by resources and guidance
- Candid teacher self-assessment and reflection
- Models of success and quality research materials readily available

The best plan for delivering professional development on learning in a classroom, in a school, or in a district includes the key factors are mentioned in the following bullet list. We found these to be successful in our training and directly correlating to key elements recognized by National Staff Development Council's (NSDC) for effective professional development:

- Share big ideas with a large group before a formal training
- Concentrate on embedded coaching of willing professionals who wish to transform teaching and learning with Inquiry
- Establish the rationale and outcomes for learners inherent in a shift to Inquiry
- Always work toward the creation of a unit plan that will actually be used in the classroom or library
- Employ the strategies of backward design, and the principles of Wiggins and McTighe, starting with the end in mind
- Generate ideas of compelling content, and target skills

EQ: Am I Ready? Do I Have Capacity for Inquiry? (*Continued*)

- Develop an overarching essential question
- Decide on a knowledge product that demonstrates new knowledge and deep understanding
- Create a summative assessment, and formative assessments in a balanced assessment plan
- Develop the strategies for instruction, activities, and collaborative practice
- Incorporate WONDER, INVESTIGATION, SYNTHESIS, and EXPRESSION

An important note is that those who benefit most from Inquiry learning are the at-risk children who cannot win when there is one right answer. The highest level of improved performance occurred with students who were not succeeding in a 20th-century style classroom where the teacher talks and students listen. Other learners benefit and excel from the natural differentiation that occurs with Inquiry. Learners usually exceed expectations in meaningful and authentic research tasks.

Wisdom for Teachers: We Hold These Truths to Be Self-Evident

- **COMPELLING CONTENT** is the meat of the lesson
- **CONNECTIONS** to prior knowledge is necessary
- QUESTIONS should be of high quality

  - Essential questions
  - Guiding questions
  - Student questions

- **THINKING** is fundamental
- **CHALLENGE** leads to depth of understanding
- **SOCIAL INTERACTION** boosts success
- **REAL-WORLD** connections are necessary for engagement
- **CHOICES** are necessary for authentic learners
- **VOICE** (student expression) is necessary for authentic learners
- **ENGAGED** learners care and count
- **COMMUNICATION** and sharing build learning communities
- **NEW KNOWLEDGE** is the goal
- **ASSESSMENT** and providing ongoing FEEDBACK are essential
- **REFLECTION and EVALUATION** are important steps for wise learners

EQ: What Is Inquiry?

Inquiry is an investigative process that engages students in developing and answering questions, solving real-world problems, confronting issues, or exploring personal interests.

- "Inquiry is a way of learning that is driven by questioning, thoughtful investigating, making sense of information, and developing new understandings. It is cyclical in nature because the result of inquiry is not simply answers but deep understandings that often lead to new questions and further pursuit of knowledge. The goal of inquiry is the exploration of significant questions and deep learning in a learner centered climate of critical engagement, social interaction, diverse information resources, and assessment to improve learning" (Barbara Stripling 1995).

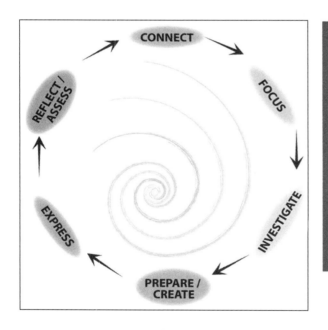

Inquiry is a cyclic and dynamic approach to learning with these steps:
- o Connect/Wonder
- o Focus/Question
- o Investigate
- o Create/Synthesize
- o Express/Communicate
- o Reflect/Assess

- **INQUIRY ignites the Common Core,** increases rigor and relevance with authentic intellectual work, engages the learner, emphasizes communication to share new knowledge, and stimulates collaboration and higher-level thinking.
- Key elements of Inquiry and the Common Core are:

QUESTIONING, SYNTHESIS, ASSESSMENT, ENGAGEMENT, BACKGROUND

BUILDING, MULTIPLE QUALITY TEXTS, and UNDERSTANDING.

- To encourage learners in an Inquiry learning environment:
  - Move beyond content coverage
  - Move beyond right answers
  - Unify with essential questions
  - Start with COMPELLING CONTENT
  - DESIGN KNOWLEDGE PRODUCTS
  - Be STUDENT CENTERED
  - Be KNOWLEDGE CENTERED
  - Be QUESTION CENTERED
  - Organize with BIG IDEAS
  - ENGAGE, ASSESS, CREATE, EXPRESS

Research correlates improved student performance with the process and products of IBL:

- **Active thinking**
- **Active learning**
- **Prior knowledge**
- **Background knowledge**
- **Choices**
- **Questions**
- **Metacognition**
- **Social interaction**
- **Depth and rigor**
- **Originality and creativity**
- **Process skills**
- **Vocabulary of the discipline**
- **Critical thinking**
- **Engaged learner**
- **Communicating and sharing**
- **Synthesis equals transfer**

This millennial generation is void of prior knowledge, and it is the prior knowledge that is needed to form the link to new knowledge. The crafters of the CCSS knew this as they shifted English Language Arts (ELA) focus toward nonfiction. From our earliest grades, teachers are now being asked to teach with nonfiction material in order to build the background knowledge so desperately needed by secondary students. Inquiry works with nonfiction and research. This book will help you understand Inquiry and how to reach students who need a personal connection to mine information and spin it into rich knowledge.

EQ: What Does Inquiry Look Like?

Teacher roles	Student roles	Disposition—engagement indicators
Well planned with the end in mind (Understanding by Design or UBD)	Willingness to work hard and collaborate	Students have a sense of "ownership"
Student centered (rather than teacher directed or teacher defined)	Tap into prior learning, that is, connections	Creativity evident
Aligned with learning objectives. Aligned with standards	Create wonder questions—What do I need to know?	Students are responsible for learning or creating
Encourage higher-level thought—plan for higher Bloom's	Investigate to answer questions and learn	Heterogeneous grouping, flexible and equitable. Students are curious and social
Real-world connections. Authentic tasks	Investigative thinkers	Collaborative—students are explorers. Students are investigators
Projects driven by essential curriculum framing questions—driving question EQ	Develop ideas in writing that go beyond the superficial	Learning displays energy in the room. Tasks are aligned with objectives
Ongoing multiple types of assessments	Brainstorm	Students use technology and share discoveries with peers
Teachers are facilitators, guides, "learning concierge"	Discovery—creativity	Students can self-assess based upon assignment, rubric, or other assessment tools
Questioning is crucial—teacher asks questions, pointedly to guide discovery	Information explorers. Research with focus	Students are looking for answers, or solving a problem, or searching for knowledge and meaning
Choice imbedded when possible	Read with focus	Interdisciplinary tasks Instructional models are interactive
Technology and thinking skills are integrated	Investigate, communicate, collaborate	Students can articulate why they are "doing" the task
Allows student "voice" and choice	Work within guidelines to tap curiosity	Students are drawing original conclusions
Embeds complexity and rigor in the task	Scrutinize information and analyze for credibility, accuracy, reliability, relevance	Students synthesize facts found
Publicly presented "product"	Present knowledge product	Communication to share knowledge
Multiple lesson types—where students will learn skills to apply	Craft written product(s)	Students see/make connections to prior knowledge
Knowledge demonstrated through *performance task or product*	Produce information	Students can articulate connections. Students use the vocabulary of the discipline

What a Traditional Instructional Model Looks Like When Inquiry Is Not Present

Students Mistakenly:

- Follow a linear process from start to finish without reflecting on success
- Seek direct answers to complex questions, rather than seeking understanding
- Copy and paste what they find from books and electronic sources
- Work to complete a task as quickly as possible
- Are relieved when the task is complete
- Value the quantity of information over quality
- View every source as valid
- Focus on the bells and whistles of the task or technology versus substance
- Work with broad inquiries and cannot "narrow" them
- Collect details without considering connections, relevance, or gaps
- Assume they can find the answer in one source and stop
- Experience no autonomy, purpose, or mastery
- Believe speed equates with intelligence
- Do not revisit assignments

Students Mistakenly Believe:

- They have to give the teacher what they want
- The point of the assignment is to get it done
- Their job is to replace mistakes with right answers
- That pride in their work is based on the grade
- School isn't supposed to relate to their lives outside of class
- That what the teacher wants them to say, is most important

Wake me when the bell rings.

Inquiry Power Grid

Transmitting to the Learner

ACTIVATE THINKING	ESSENTIAL Questions	Student Centered
WONDER	Guiding Questions	Social Interaction
CURIOSITY	FOCUS Questions	Substantive Conversation
Prior knowledge	Learner generated questions	ENGAGED Learner
Build background	Authentic Tasks	Formative Assessment ongoing
Vocabulary/Word Wall	Meaningful audience	Peer review
BIG IDEAS	Knowledge product	CRITICAL engagement
CHOICES	Construct meaning	CRITICAL THINKING
MEANING	Synthesize	TECHNOLOGY
REAL WORLD	COMMUNICATE/SHARE	PRODUCE

2

Inquiry in Action

We learn more by looking for the answer to a question and not finding it than we do from learning the answer itself.

—Lloyd Alexander

EQ: What Are the Pedagogy Verbs for Inquiry?

When teachers are trapped in a direct instruction model, their pedagogy consists of:

- Lectures
- Question and answers
- Imbedded video, pictures, worksheets
- Quizzes, tests
- "Projects"—well defined by the teacher, and more

If you examine the Inquiry model, you will see that the pedagogy is "rich" with a plethora of instructional verbs that can be broken down into our four stages of Inquiry: Wonder, Identify, Synthesize, and Express. A teacher, who is familiar with many of these verbs, will not have a difficult time switching instruction to an Inquiry model. In fact, teachers are likely to find they are doing "pieces" of Inquiry independently, outside the framework of a true Inquiry model. Therefore, a switch to an Inquiry-based model can be a small change with a large engagement effect.

Educators often remark, "This is how I used to teach fifteen years ago—BA—before assessment." Examine the pedagogy verb shere, which were extrapolated from the Common Core, and highlight what you currently embrace in your instruction.

Integrate	Critique
Evaluate	Analyze—think analytically
Comprehend	Address a question
Solve a problem	Integrate information avoiding plagiarism
Conduct short research projects	Produce and publish writing
Conduct sustained research projects	Interact and collaborate
Students generate questions	Debate
Explore a topic	Write arguments to support claims
Draw evidence from texts	Formulate an argument
Support analysis	Comprehend
Research and reflect	Prepare and participate effectively in conversations
Gather information from print and digital sources	Build and express persuasively
Assess the credibility and accuracy of sources	Express information and enhance understanding

EQ: What Are the Pedagogy Verbs for Inquiry? (*Continued*)

When the crafters of the Common Core Standards (CCS) attempted to redefine education for global competitiveness, they knew educators had to raise the level of thought throughout America. As Lily Ekelson, Vice President of the National Education Association at the time of the Common Core introduction said, "We don't live in a multiple choice world."

There are two parts to the Common Core: content and pedagogy. To ignore the pedagogical shifts and remain in silos with shut doors, lecturing to students, defeats the purpose the CCS is advancing. If you embrace most of these, you will likely find your students in the library hunting down information so that they *can research to build and present knowledge.*

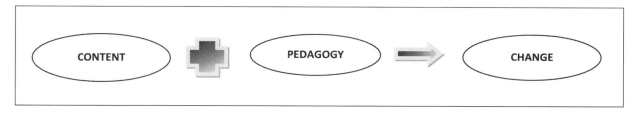

EQ: How Does Inquiry Benefit the Learner?

A fourth grader named Taylor pursued an Inquiry-based project sparked by a Junior Great Books story. His personal investigation, question, and original product, delighted Taylor and those who guided him in the process. His statement to his teacher captured the value of Inquiry for him: "When I am in the classroom, there is always just one right answer. But when I do an inquiry, I feel my mind fly like an eagle."

A seventh grader who faced challenges with rote learning, engaged with her peers in a highly interdisciplinary Inquiry based on the holocaust. This student had a choice and a voice in the project. Inquiry projects were initiated after careful background building experiences, discussions, and question development. Reading complex texts beyond grade level, this girl delved into the harsh realities of Auschwitz with stamina and empathy. She showcased her deep understanding of the experience of this Nazi Concentration Camp in a six-by-eight-foot mural, alive with feeling tone and careful detail. In the blue and lavender tones that captured the smoke emitted by the crematoria, this young learner excelled in her conceptual grasp of the history beyond the expectations of her teachers and special educators.

Inquiry has deep roots in brain research. Understanding how kids learn is the basis for effective pedagogy. Many instructional practices ignore brain research, and get poor results. Passive learners who listen to learn retain very little of what they hear, perhaps as little as 5% after two weeks. Active learners engaged in Inquiry achieve long-term understanding of content. Learning characterized by background building, attention to prior knowledge, questioning, investigation, original conclusions, synthesis, and communication results in lasting and flexible new knowledge. Inquiry as a model of instruction is brain based.

Curiosity, personal connections to content, real-world problem solving, and collaboration stimulate successful learners. Rote learning can downgrade to a functional scoop-and-spit cycle, where the learner completes a necessary task of retrieving, recording, and restating with no meaning. Constructing meaning from texts, disciplined Inquiry with multiple sources of information, and connections beyond the school are at the heart of Inquiry-driven instruction and positive learning outcomes. *Information Power* embraced these principles in 1998, and they continue to resonate in many studies about optimizing outcomes for learners.

Inquiry departs from the prescribed sequence of a teacher-directed lesson. Curricular content connects to the learner with meaning and questions. Big ideas evolve that become a matrix for authentic focus and investigation by the learner. Using quality texts to build meaning, the learner experiences personal efficacy. The power of motivation transports the learner to close reading of complex text. Rigor and relevance are at the heart of the Common Core. With purpose and support in mastering necessary skills, even at-risk learners are motivated by meaningful rigorous work. Studies in Ontario and Chicago with at-risk learners concluded that making work harder not easier improved performance.

Inquiry is rich with social interaction, relationships, and ongoing conversation. These impact the retention of new knowledge. Using, manipulating, and applying new learning also contribute to moving ideas from short-term recall to formative knowledge. Formative knowledge is a foundation. It is the building block of expanded understanding, connections, and creativity. An inherent sense of ownership results from Inquiry learning. Engaged learners experience community and critical response when they are thinking, problem solving, and sharing. The student is learning how to learn.

College and career readiness extends beyond knowledge and skill to key behaviors and attitudes. Noncognitive skills and emotional intelligence help students to transition to higher education and the world of work. Persistence, independence, resiliency, confidence, self-awareness, and motivation are powerful agents that contribute to success. Ultimately the path to the Common Core is Inquiry.

EQ: How Can I Advocate
for Better Research in My School?

The Common Core does not say "Fetch!" College and career readiness does not happen with worksheets, scoop-and-spit reports, transfer of facts from source to packet, or any manifestation of low-level "research" projects. These often unproductive activities consume learning time and energy. Allison Zmuda, a national expert on school improvement, asks bluntly, "Why bother?"

Ironically, the fact fetching is actually an integral part of building new knowledge and deep understanding, but with real meaning, vocabulary development, and close reading. Teachers, school librarians, administrators, literacy coaches, and subject area experts need to work together to move beyond fact gathering to building new knowledge with texts. A shift to student-centered rather than task-driven action is key. This happens when the student knows "why" he is investigating and discovering meaning and answers. This will foster ownership and original conclusions.

Consider this as a reality check. Students arrive in school libraries with "packets" that merely require *Hide 'n Seek* for facts. Bureaucratic tasks generate bureaucratic behavior and results. How many times has a student asked the fatal question: "Is this enough?" "How many sentences do you want?" "Is this what you want?" How many capable young learners simply seek the shortest distance between two points? How many play the game, check off the jobs to be accomplished, then copy, cut, and paste, or plug bits of information into a topical litany? Most importantly, how many could converse knowingly about that topic two weeks after it is neat and complete? How many would connect that topic to new learning at a later time? Research states—almost none. Why bother?

The Common Core does not say stockpile or squirrel away facts. All educators are in a place where critical eyes review routine or comfortable practice. Starting a conversation about improving a lesson with Common Core Shifts, or rigorous standards is everyone's responsibility. See something, say something might apply here in a high-stakes learning environment. Teachers working together always achieve a better outcome than teachers working in isolation. Research on collaborative practice bears this out.

If you examine the pedagogy verbs of the Common Core, you will see that they all require higher-level thought and an element of interaction with facts or *evidence from the text.* Knowing that premise should give librarians and teachers the basis for:

- Taking a stand against low-level projects. Time is too valuable to waste with *Information Hide 'n Seek.*
- Advocating for higher-level thought to require students to "do something with those facts."

- Standing firm on their commitment to repackage delivery for the sake of learners.
- Encouraging teachers to align their educational endeavors to the Common Core State Standards (CCSS).

Have the repackaging recipe ready:
- Content defined
- EQ for the student to investigate
- Information sources agreed to by librarian and teacher together
- Search Process—easy four-step process laid out by librarian

  - Know what you are looking for
  - Identify search terms
  - Investigate—Locate sources (and evaluate if necessary)
  - Take notes in your own words, bullets, and use the (locally defined) tools available

- Wrap up EQ answer in a knowledge product.

Heaven help us all, if the next generation does not learn how to think. Every time students embark on *Info Hide 'n Seek,* they are missing an opportunity to grow their brain and letting a computer think for them. Aldous Huxley predicted this in the 1940s when he claimed *people will come to love technologies that undue their capacity to think* (Huxley 1946). When we were young, we had to be taught how to find information. That is no longer the case. We have to rise above merely finding information and teach students how to evaluate and use information.

Most administrators are well trained in pedagogy and characteristics of good teaching. They are required to evaluate teachers from the eyes of Danielson, Marzano, and other people who have well defined the characteristics of good instruction. Therefore, librarians or teachers are on solid ground to have a frank discussion with their principal or curriculum administrator.

Diplomatically, an educator could package this concern with the following thoughts:

- The Common Core advocates for higher-level thought.
- The Common Core advocates for collaborative projects and I believe that many research units could be improved by a simple planning meeting to address:

  - The need to move beyond finding facts to synthesis.
  - Adopting a litmus test for higher-level thought: *Is this assignment answerable on Google?* If so, it *requires* repackaging.

EQ: How Can I Advocate for Better Research in My School? (*Continued*)

- The possibility of adopting a simple building-wide research model aligned with CCSS expectations of (CCSS Writing Standard 8) citing sources, writing from evidence, and avoiding plagiarism. (Have the WISE model ready.)

Remember less is more, when dealing with administrators. Succinctly package your message into carefully crafted sentences and slogans easily remembered. As Alison Zmuda says, "Administrators don't want to hear you whine. They want to hear simple suggestions to any simple problem you present."

EQ: How Do I Create an Evidence-Based Plan for Inquiry?

Think of Teachers As:

- Content framers
- Coaches
- Guides
- Listeners
- Motivators of curiosity
- Conference partners
- Background builders
- Questioners
- Monitors
- Encouragers
- Communicators
- Target skill teacher
- Continuous assessors

Think of Kids As:

- Explorers
- Problem solvers
- Cognitive apprentices
- Discoverers
- Innovators
- Questioners
- Producers of knowledge
- Thinkers
- Communicators
- Collaborators

Consider:

In the Beginning

- Backward design
- Compelling, rich content
- Unifying essential questions
- Driven by student questions
- Collaborative design, question development
- Authentic, real world purpose, audience
- KNOWLEDGE PRODUCT
- Goal of deep understanding
- Rigor and challenge

Early in the Process

- Background building
- Vocabulary development
- Prior knowledge and experience
- Prior attitudes
- Student questioning
- MEANING
- Choices
- Ongoing formative assessment
- Teacher as guide, coach, facilitator
- Social interaction

Information to Knowledge Journey

- Construction of meaning
- Learning to learn

Important Constants

- Thinking, original conclusions
- Synthesis

EQ: How Do I Create an Evidence-Based Plan for Inquiry? (*Continued*)

- Investigation using quality resources
- Student centered
- Engaged learner
- Authentic intellectual work
- Connections to text, self, and world
- Skill development, improved performance
- Sustained dialog and feedback

AND

- Intellectual support system
- Emotion
- Creativity
- Knowledge use, knowledge creation
- Disseminating, sharing products
- Communicating to share knowledge
- 21st-Century Skills

- Reflection, metacognition
- Active learner, discovering and linking ideas
- Collaboration—students and teachers
- Elaborated communication
- Problem solving
- Sharing of products
- Critical engagement

RX Self-assessment break:

Do you see evidence of these in your planning?

Planning Inquiry to Foster Student Ownership

WHAT is the compelling content?	
HOW will we ACTIVATE thinking?	
HOW will we build background info and connect to prior knowledge?	
HOW will we make our plan STUDENT CENTERED?	
HOW will the students reflect deep understanding and master content?	
HOW will we pre-assess?	
How will we use summative assessment?	
HOW will we use formative assessment?	
EQ: How does the Essential Question guide deepen understanding?	
WHERE will students find information?	
WHAT will students do with the information?	
WHEN are students expected to complete the inquiry?	
HOW will students share their products with meaningful audiences?	

From *Rx for the Common Core: Toolkit for Implementing Inquiry Learning* by Mary Boyd Ratzer and Paige Jaeger. Santa Barbara, CA: Libraries Unlimited. Copyright © 2014.

EQ: Why Does Backward Design Work?

In light of 21st-century learners and the Common Core, planning a lesson or unit, has evolved into a process requiring skill and pedagogical expertise. It is not acceptable to just continue instruction with old status quo lesson plans. A few notes in a plan book, or even a reasonably complete lesson, are no longer sufficient. Teaching is no longer a creative art, but is now a data-driven science, carefully planned and aligned with learning targets.

Understanding by Design by Wiggins and McTighe, and the highly effective influence of *backward design,* have propelled lesson planning into a thoughtful, disciplined craft. Lesson planning now must consider:

- compelling content,
- essential understandings and essential questions,
- vocabulary of the discipline,
- balanced assessment,
- motivational considerations,
- focused performance indicators,
- standards,
- differentiation,
- accommodations,
- scaffolding, and
- knowledge products,

All of these lesson planning considerations rocket educators to new levels of professionalism. The quality plan drives the engine of instructional success. Planning for Inquiry starts almost always with a *compelling content.* Teachers should:

- Survey the curricular landscape and select the very important, central, engaging, and sufficiently complex piece of content as the primary content.
- Consider the essential question as the frame for the lesson—a frame that will sustain higher-level thinking, questioning, and student work.
- Early on, generate real world connections between the learning and the learner to define the relevance.
- Build background knowledge, elicit prior knowledge, and generate curiosity.
- Craft the lesson from the EQ in a logical progression to a knowledge product, which demonstrates genuine understanding.
- Plan for formative assessment, reflection, and self-assessment as well as social interaction to document learning and increase student participation in the learning process.
- Model transparent thinking and metacognition where and when appropriate to teach kids how to think.

EQ: Why Does Backward Design Work? (*Continued*)

- Embrace depth and rigor, and consider the different needs of students in the process.
- Plan for summative assessment, which involves sharing with a meaningful audience to complete the circle.

This formula for planning comes together in the field-tested planning tools that follow.

ROADMAP FOR PLANNING A COLLABORATIVE RESEARCH UNIT

Information-Infused Investigation

Librarian and classroom teacher do the work

1. **Begin with the end in mind** (backward design, Wiggins & McTighe): Collaborate with teachers in planning, if possible.

   - What do you want your students to know when they are finished?
   - What is the core content?
   - What is (are) the *Common Core* learning standards I want to hit?
   - What information literacy (IL) skills will you focus on during this unit?
     AASL 21st-Century Standards
     ISTE Standards (if your school has embraced these)

2. Identify essential vocabulary of the discipline:
   Teacher(s) provides—needed for assessment, useful for research, would like to see used in writing, discussion and research.

3. Teacher "sets the stage":

   - How will I introduce this project?
   - What background knowledge do students need?
   - Do I need to preteach essential background? Skills?

4. Develop the investigation's "big question" so that the project inspires student learning/interest.

5. Plan and deliver preassessment strategies:

   - Classroom teacher's content
   - Librarian's preassessment of IL skills
   - Librarian identifies:
     - IL skills needed
     - EQs for instruction
     - Resource potential

Students do the work

6. Students:

   - Generate research questions
   - Activate thinking
     - Embed meaning,
     - Connect to student's world

7. Research . . . investigation

   - What resources will students use?
   - Websites, books, databases, etc.

8. What is the final (knowledge) project?

Teachers and students

9. How will I assess student learning?
   Reflect on the process when the unit is complete
   What will I do differently next time?

From *Rx for the Common Core: Toolkit for Implementing Inquiry Learning* by Mary Boyd Ratzer and Paige Jaeger. Santa Barbara, CA: Libraries Unlimited. Copyright © 2014.

EQ: How Do *Essential Questions* Redirect Learning?

EQs capture the significance and *meaning* of a curriculum unit. They encompass the many relevant guiding questions used to build understanding into a BIG IDEA. These questions propel learning to the highest levels of Bloom's Taxonomy and **unify all teacher actions** to result in **deep understanding** of the content.

EQs drive rigor and depth because they move beyond the collection of discreet facts and demand synthesis from the learner. These questions promote critical thinking and the building of conceptual knowledge.

EQs can be used as pre- and post-assessment tools. A student should not be able to answer the essential question at the beginning of a unit, but should be able to articulate the answer with meaningful understanding and discussion at the end.

Characteristics of Good EQs:

- Are arguable and important
- Are at the heart of the subject
- Often start with HOW? WHY? WHICH? WHAT IF? SHOULD? SO WHAT?
- Recur in school and in life
- Raise more questions
- Often raise important issues
- Can provide a purpose for learning
- Move students beyond understanding and studying and require a conclusion, a resolution or action, a choice, a decision, or an opinion to be supported with evidence
- Cannot be answered in a few words such as a "yes" or a "no"

EQ: How Do *Essential Questions* Redirect Learning? (*Continued*)

- Probably shift and evolve
- May be unanswerable
- Will serve as a unifying core for a plan

The ability to craft essential questions that drive deep content discovery is a difficult skill, initially. The more an educator tries this approach, the easier it gets. In fact, if teachers work together as a grade-level team, curriculum team, or team with their librarian, they are likely to brainstorm a better essential question than they would on their own. Two or more heads are better than one.

Review the following questions to see how a simple overarching question can be created to embrace many other smaller reading and research tasks, fostering deep understanding. These questions are samples from both the elementary and secondary levels. Can you guess which level and curriculum topic they would embrace?

EQ: How Do *Essential Questions* Redirect Learning? (*Continued*)

EQ Sampler—Consider their impact on *how* a unit is taught.

- How did the actions and beliefs of individuals sustain the Union from 1861 to 1865?
- How would a rock tell its life story?
- How do numbers define wellness?
- How does energy define the quality of life past, present, and future?
- Why war?
- What should be the Bill of Rights for South Sudan, Mali, or Afghanistan?
- How does the Iroquois way of life demonstrate principles that 21st-century civilization needs to consider?
- How does interdependence impact the terrestrial ecology?
- Why do civilizations fail?
- Why do democracies fail?
- Why should the rainforest be saved for any one of the species that live there?
- How do communities provide for wants and needs in different geographic regions of the earth?
- How did Jim Crow create a pre-Civil War reality for African Americans?
- How did climate and weather create the Dust Bowl? Why could that disaster recur?
- What if a country of your choice were a village? How can mathematic proportions and demographics represent social groups, religions, economics, resources, and the relationship of population to geography?
- How can statistics lie?
- Why do holocausts continue to generate hatred, oppression, and violence?
- Do military generals make good U.S. presidents?
- How did the Industrial Revolution affect children and families?
- Why does the *Sun* deserve the *Golden Globe Award*?
- Forensic footprints: What type of footprint did your (biography) leave behind?
- What would your president say to America today?
- Based on data, for what kind of funding or support would your country's ambassador plead to the United Nations?
- Are our U.S. states mutually interdependent? What are the imports and exports for your U.S. state? What are the promises and perils of your U.S. state?

From *Rx for the Common Core: Toolkit for Implementing Inquiry Learning* by Mary Boyd Ratzer and Paige Jaeger. Santa Barbara, CA: Libraries Unlimited. Copyright © 2014.

EQ: How Do I Self-Assess Inquiry-Based Plans?

Inquiry Planning Checklist

Review this checklist as a goal setting activity. Highlight the boxes that are part of your Inquiry lesson plan. Think about how can they empower the learner to say, "**I care. I count. I can.**" Which are most important to successful learners?

Inquiry dynamics: strategies, skills, practices	Part of our plan	Very important
Background knowledge		
Prior knowledge, experience		
EQs		
Questions developed by the learner		
Choices, focus		
Engagement, emotion		
Student-centered process		
Student-negotiated process, products		
Backwards design		
Social interaction		
Compelling content		
Investigation using quality information		
Product is evidence of new knowledge		
Synthesis of multiple information sources		
Meaning constructed		
Information to knowledge journey		
Reflection, metacognition		
Depth, rigor, challenge		
Understanding, formative knowledge		
Collaboration—student and teachers		
Communication to share knowledge		
21st-Century Skills		
Thinking, original conclusions		
Ongoing formative assessment		
Learning to learn		
Content mastery		

From *Rx for the Common Core: Toolkit for Implementing Inquiry Learning* by Mary Boyd Ratzer and Paige Jaeger. Santa Barbara, CA: Libraries Unlimited. Copyright © 2014.

Assessing Teaching Practice, Inquiry Planning, Unit Plans

As I Teach, I Should Self-Assess

Have I...

- Determined and communicated learning goals for higher-order thinking skills?
- Addressed learning standards? Rigor?
- Tapped prior knowledge and built background?
- Emphasized connections, explicit or inferred?
- Promoted student thinking?
  - Interpreting facts
  - Synthesizing information
  - Reasoning logically
  - Framing arguments with evidence
- Promoted student questioning? Deep levels of questioning?
- Used organization tools, mapping, charts, timelines?
- Developed criteria for evaluating information, relative importance and relevance of ideas?
- Engendered debate and discussion?
- Focused on essential question and focus questions?
- Provided paths to investigation? Choices?
- Mentored and guided self-directed students?
- Promoted active, authentic quest for new ideas authentic questions, resources, products?
- Integrated original conclusions?
  - Test against evidence
  - Divergent/convergent thinking
  - Relative strength of arguments, positions, perspectives
  - Critical stance
- Planned and implemented multiple, ongoing assessments?
- Incorporated technology?
- Framed a final knowledge product that is publicly presented?
- Utilized models and criteria in advance?

Have I . . .

- Determined and communicated learning goals for higher-order thinking skills?

- Addressed learning standards? Rigor?

- Tapped prior knowledge and built background?

- Emphasized connections, explicit or inferred?

- Promoted student thinking?

  - Interpreting facts
  - Synthesizing information
  - Reasoning logically
  - Framing arguments with evidence

- Promoted student questioning? Deep levels of questioning?

- Used organizational tools, mapping, charts, timelines?

- Developed criteria for evaluating information, relative importance, and relevance of ideas?

- Engendered debate and discussion?

- Focused on essential question and focus questions?

- Provided paths to investigation? Choices?

- Mentored and guided self-directed students?

- Promoted active, authentic quest for new ideas authentic questions, resources, products?

- Integrated original conclusions?

  - Test against evidence
  - Divergent/convergent thinking
  - Relative strength of arguments, positions, perspectives
  - Critical stance

- Planned and implemented multiple, ongoing assessments?

- Incorporated technology?

- Framed a final knowledge product that is publicly presented?

- Utilized models and criteria in advance?

3

Inquiry and the Common Core

A mind is a fire to be kindled, not a vessel to be filled.

—Plutarch

EQ: How Does the Common Core Embrace Research?

When research starts with a question, the task is presented as a quest—a problem that must be solved. This fosters "ownership" in the process and allows the students to use information sources they are familiar with—bait 'n switch—Voila! Eventually, they realize that after they have insufficiently gleaned sources from their "mode of choice," they will recognize that they need to dig deeper into the credible, authoritative, reliable, sources they will need to build up, back up, and support their position. You have fostered ownership and responsibility.

In an Inquiry format, students are given a "voice," a choice, and an opportunity to personalize the learning experience digging for answers that are meaningful and relevant to their life. If they don't care, they won't achieve. Therein lies the relevance emphasized in the CCS.

Millennial students are operating in a new mode of transliteracy—they read, uncover, and discover through a myriad of mediums. There is often no longer a *structure* to reading and research. Students will read, watch, extract words, and synthesize from a variety of sources and source types. It is so imperative that we as learning concierges are able to guide students through the process of discovering meaning and drawing conclusions. This Inquiry process promotes higher-level thought, is aligned with the Common Core, replicates real-world problem solving strategies, and engages the students.

In Appendix A of the Common Core, there is one paragraph that acknowledges that this generation, the millennials, gravitate to text-free or text-light sources:

> *If students cannot read challenging texts with understanding—if they have not developed the skill, concentration, and stamina to read such texts—they will read less in general. In particular, if students cannot read complex expository text to gain information, they will likely turn to text-free or text-light sources, such as video, podcasts, and tweets. These sources, while not without value, cannot capture the nuance, subtlety, depth, or breadth of ideas developed through complex text.* (CCSS—Appendix A: p. 4; italics added for emphasis)

In an Inquiry model, we can start where they are, build background information in their "literacy mode of choice," and move them to rigorous sources that challenge and hold gold.

This millennial generation who have spent years watching television and playing video games is void of "prior knowledge." Rote teaching of content has left little in students' long-term memory. Brain research suggests that for new knowledge to make it to the long-term file cabinet, it has to be linked to prior knowledge. However, if the cabinet is empty—a big vacancy of knowledge—there's nothing to connect to. The crafters of the Common Core State Standards (CCSS) knew this, as they shifted English Language Arts (ELA) focus toward nonfiction at the earliest grades. Teachers are now being asked to teach with nonfiction material in order to build the background knowledge so desperately needed in the secondary students. Inquiry supports this goal.

EQ: How Can I Compare My Plan to the Common Core?

Aligning instruction to the Common Core is more than just checking off a standard. It includes a paradigm change in instructional models. At the very core, there is a shift to student-centered learning—rather than teacher-directed delivery. That is not to say that there won't be an opportunity for "direct instruction." The change states that entire direct instruction must be reevaluated and realigned.

Content + Delivery change = Common Core change

If you want students	Common Core says
Who are college and career ready in reading, writing, speaking, and listening	• Build strong content knowledge • Demonstrate independence • Respond to varying demand of audience, task, purpose, and discipline • Comprehend as well as critique • Value evidence • Use technology and digital media strategically and capably
To integrate knowledge and ideas	• Use their experience and their knowledge and logic to think analytically, address problems creatively, and advocate persuasively • Integrate and evaluate multiple sources of information presented in different media or formats to address a question or solve a problem
To research to build and present knowledge	• Conduct short as well as more sustained research projects to answer a question (including self-generated questions) • Draw on several sources and related focused questions that allow for multiple avenues of exploration • Develop factual, interpretive, and evaluative questions for further exploration of the topic • Draw evidence from literary or informational texts to support analysis reflection and research • Gather relevant information from multiple print and digital sources • Assess the credibility and accuracy of each source • Integrate the information avoiding plagiarism
Produce and distribute writing	• Use technology, including the Internet, to product and publish writing and to interact and collaborate with others • Write arguments to support claims in an analysis of substantive topics or texts using valid reasoning and relevant and sufficient texts • Explore and inquire into areas of interest to formulate an argument

(Continued)

EQ: How Can I Compare My Plan to the Common Core? (*Continued*)

If you want students	Common Core says
Comprehend and collaboration	• Prepare for and participate effectively in a range of conversations and collaborations with diverse partners, building on the other's ideas and expressing their own ideas clearly and persuasively • Integrate and evaluate information presented in diverse media formats—visually, quantitatively, and orally
Presentation of knowledge and ideas	• Present information, finding, and supporting evidence such that listeners can follow the line of reasoning and the organization, development, and style are appropriate to the task, purpose, and audience • Make strategic use of digital media and visual displays of data to express information and enhance understanding

See Appendix for sample CCSS & Inquiry planning template

EQ: How Does Inquiry Affect Rigor and Relevance?

The Common Core Learning Standards are rigorous. A sampling of expectations from the Common Core Standards, listed in this chapter, affirms a commitment to rigor. The economy requires college and career-ready graduates equipped with the level of competency stated in these high school expectations. Relevance is also significant as learners develop questions, see connections between content and their real world, find their voice, and explore perspectives. Mastery of content knowledge and deep understanding are the stated outcomes of Inquiry and the Common Core. Essentially, *Inquiry energizes spinning the straw of found facts into the gold of new understanding, original conclusions, and new perspectives.*

A reality check reveals the need for teachers to shift from low level: fill in the blank worksheets; fact-finding projects that only transfer information from textbooks; passive learners listening to content coverage; and other teacher-directed tasks. Practices such as these generate a short-term recall of facts and a familiarity with content—both of which are quickly forgotten. Long-term retention and deep, formative knowledge that can be transferred to new learning require a *synthesis* of what is found in research projects. Transforming discreet bits of information from sources requires:

- *connecting* related details,
- generating big ideas,
- weighing authority, importance, relevance, and use

Beginning with essential questions and learning targets, **teachers** establish goals that are rigorous.

Beginning with prior knowledge, background building, and the vocabulary of the discipline, **learners** observe, develop questions, and build meaning early in the process. With a focus on relevant and compelling content, the **learner** generates questions that are high level, woven with a grasp of who, what, where, and when of new content. Progressing from recall and rote, the **learner** sets a target for research that is meaningful and complex. How? Why? Should? What if?

In Inquiry and the Common Core, *learners* thoughtfully negotiate multiple perspectives, oppositional positions, information gaps, varying levels of authority, fact and opinion, and primary and secondary sources. They bridge the gap between short-term recall and deep understanding. *Learners* articulating new understanding in written arguments, discussions, and debates access their core ideas flexibly and in relation to one another. *Learners* prioritize, revise, extend, and self-assess. Their ownership of original knowledge products and ideas manifests itself in effort and quality. Collaborating and sharing products using technology enhance critical review and analysis. Rigor and relevance live!

EQ: How Does Inquiry Affect Rigor and Relevance? (*Continued*)

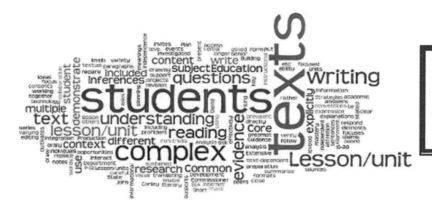

Wordle:

New York Education Commissioner's Expectations for Common Core Lessons

A Sample of Rigorous and Relevant Common Core Expectations

The Common Core has been examined, debated, and digested in pieces. The premise of the Common Core was to raise college and career readiness through rigor. Inquiry-based research projects are one way to elevate the rigor of yesterday's simplistic research projects. Examine the statements below from the CCSS standards that demonstrate the paradigm shift to student-centered research and student empowerment through information. These are rigorous indeed. The day of research projects easily answered on Google is over.

- Write arguments to support claims in an analysis using valid reasoning and relevant and sufficient evidence. Explore and inquire into areas of interest to formulate an argument.

- Introduce precise, knowledgeable claim(s), establish the significance of the claim(s), distinguish the claim(s) from alternate or opposing claims, and create an organization that logically sequences claim(s), counterclaims, reasons, and evidence.

- Develop claim(s) and counterclaims supplying the most relevant evidence for each, while pointing out the strengths and limitations of both, in a manner that anticipates the audience's knowledge level, concerns, values, and possible biases.

- Produce clear and coherent writing in which the development, organization, and style are appropriate to task, purpose, and audience.

- Conduct short as well as more sustained research projects to answer a question (including a self-generated question) or solve a problem; narrow or broaden the Inquiry when appropriate; synthesize multiple sources on the subject, demonstrating understanding of the subject under investigation.

EQ: How Does Inquiry Affect Rigor and Relevance? (*Continued*)

- Gather relevant information from multiple authoritative print and digital sources, using advanced searches effectively; assess the strengths and limitations of each source in terms of the task, purpose, and audience; integrate information into the text selectively to maintain the flow of ideas, avoiding plagiarism and overreliance on any one source and following a standard format for citation.

- Engage effectively in a range of collaborative discussions (one-on-one, in groups, and teacher led) with diverse partners on *grade 8 topics, texts, and issues,* building on others' ideas and expressing their own clearly.

- Come to discussions prepared, having read or researched material under study; explicitly draw on that preparation by referring to evidence on the topic, text, or issue to probe and reflect on ideas under discussion.

- Use their experience and their knowledge of language and logic, as well as culture, to think analytically, address problems creatively, and advocate persuasively.

- Present claims and findings, emphasizing salient points in a focused, coherent manner with relevant evidence, sound valid reasoning, and well-chosen details; use appropriate eye contact, adequate volume, and clear pronunciation.

- Propel conversations by posing and responding to questions that probe reasoning and evidence; ensure a hearing for a full range of positions on a topic or issue; clarify, verify, or challenge ideas and conclusions; and promote divergent and creative perspectives.

- Respond thoughtfully to diverse perspectives; synthesize comments, claims, and evidence made on all sides of an issue; resolve contradictions when possible; and determine what additional information or research is required to deepen the investigation or complete the task.

- Describe the connection between a series of historical events, scientific ideas or concepts, or steps in technical procedures in a text.

- Develop factual, interpretive, and evaluative questions for further exploration of the topic(s).

- Synthesize information from a range of sources (e.g., texts, experiments, simulations) into a coherent understanding of a process, phenomenon, or concept, resolving conflicting information when possible (Corestandards.org).

Common Core Power Grid

This research-based self-assessment tool is a quick guide to check for instructional elements of the CCSS in a lesson plan

Rigor	Evidence	Argument
ACTIVATE THINKING	ESSENTIAL Questions	Build Independence
CONNECTIONS	Target standards skills	Social Interaction, conversation
Collaboration	FOCUS Questions	Close Reading
Connect with Prior knowledge	Learner generated questions	ENGAGED Learner
Build Background	Authentic Tasks Models	Formative Assessment ongoing
Develop Academic Vocabulary	Meaningful audience, task, purpose	Peer review Self-assessment
BIG IDEAS	Knowledge product	CRITICAL engagement
CHOICES	Construct meaning from text	CRITICAL THINKING, problem solving
Perspectives	Synthesize	TECHNOLOGY and Digital Media
REAL WORLD through text	COMMUNICATE SHARE	PRODUCE
RELEVANCE	Writing Speaking	TEXTS

Set goals for your Common Core learning experience by plugging in the *essential elements* of INQUIRY. Highlight in the grid and then check for KNOWLEDGE POWER in your plan.

EQ: How Does the Common Core and Inquiry Empower the Learner for Rigorous Work?

Recently during professional development, a teacher said she was "doing" the Common Core. She was in fact, just treating it as a new checklist where she must "do" a close reading; "do" an evidence-based writing task; identify the vocabulary of the discipline, and so on. We also believe teachers think, "If we increase rigor in our current ELA novels, we'll be aligned."

We wish the instructional paradigm shift in the CCSS was so easy. The rigor in the Common Core is to foster intelligence and achievement. The relevance in the Common Core is to foster motivation in this millennial generation. We like to tell students that these lessons will make them smarter, richer, and more successful in life. The body of research on the millennials speaks to the fact they want to know why they must "do" something. That is why Inquiry works. That is why the Common Core says rigor and relevance.

Empower the Learner

If your formative assessment is in first person language (i.e., I can…), then the responsibility is transferred to the student. If a student is given individual choice in either a topic, knowledge product, thesis, or conclusion, then the assignment is "owned" by the student and the student is "empowered."

The greater relevance an assignment has to the learner's real world, the greater the motivation and the greater the "transfer" of responsibility (i.e., buy-in) for completion. We call this empowering the learner. Even a difficult assignment such as a close reading task can become student centered, if the "task" allows for individual interpretation, discussion, or Inquiry.

EQ: How Does the Common Core and Inquiry Empower the Learner for Rigorous Work? (*Continued*)

Librarians can suggest that teachers follow a close reading lesson or other classroom activity with a "short- or long-term" research task to continue the learning and allow for student discovery. If students are allowed to create their own questions for further investigation, they own the activity.

The schematic representation that follows is a picture of a Common Core lesson. Please note the inclusion of a research task. This is to embrace the Writing Standards 6,7,8,9, which say students should "research to build and present knowledge." All too often, teachers stop at the close reading task, and do not follow the "read" up with a task to make it "relevant." Why just read a primary source or "rich text," when this could be coupled with a "short- or long-term research" task that gives the students an opportunity to dig deeper, conclude, synthesize, form opinions linked to evidence, and other higher-level-thought Common Core tasks.

Common Core Recipe

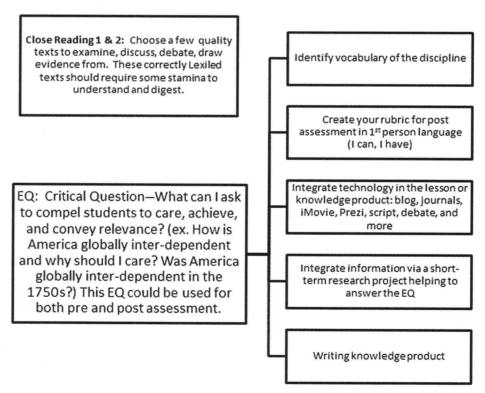

Close Reading 1 & 2: Choose a few quality texts to examine, discuss, debate, draw evidence from. These correctly Lexiled texts should require some stamina to understand and digest.

EQ: Critical Question—What can I ask to compel students to care, achieve, and convey relevance? (ex. How is America globally inter-dependent and why should I care? Was America globally inter-dependent in the 1750s?) This EQ could be used for both pre and post assessment.

Identify vocabulary of the discipline

Create your rubric for post assessment in 1st person language (I can, I have)

Integrate technology in the lesson or knowledge product: blog, journals, iMovie, Prezi, script, debate, and more

Integrate information via a short-term research project helping to answer the EQ

Writing knowledge product

EQ: How Does a Knowledge Product Differ from an Information Product?

The Common Core states that students should "Research to Build and Present Knowledge." At the very core, the assumption is this is *knowledge*—something they know, hold dearly in their brain, have synthesized, and are sharing with an audience. To report *only information* suggests "This is what I have found; I don't necessarily care about this; it was required of me, and I'm done."

Examine the following characteristics to assess whether your assignments fall into one category or the other.

As you plan your unit, a task for *synthesis* must be imbedded to set the project apart from low-level fact recall assignments. This requires three essential pieces:

1. An essential question that must be answered,

2. A real-world link that fosters relevance to the learner, and

3. A "presentation" or "package" (technology infused or performance task) that demonstrates the knowledge, rather than merely "reporting" it.

Information products	Knowledge products
• Use simple search strategies	• Require students identify issues or concepts
• Focus on facts	• Require students to frame arguments
• Reflect squirreling or fact stockpiling	• Require students to determine points that must be explored for evidence
• Result in no change in long-term knowledge	• Require students to become content experts as they probe
• Use the easiest part of the search process—availability of information	• Require relationships in ideas—connections
• Reflect low levels of interest or engagement	• Have used rich information sources
• Resemble a bureaucratic task	• Provoke deep thought
• Are missing pieces of the "whole story"	• Prompt analysis of facts
• Reflect Information overload	• Enable personal understanding, demonstrate deep knowledge
• Little evaluation is present—passive reception	• Encourage transfer of facts into memory
• Rarely link to background knowledge or prior knowledge	• Deliver a message of deep understanding
• Reflect a student's inability to reduce and manage information	• Reflect originality
• Require little evaluation	• Support the Common Core
• Foster relief when the project is over	• Give direction to the project
	• Need an audience for presentation

EQ: How Does a Knowledge Product Differ from An Information Product? (*Continued*)

KNOWLEDGE Product Design—Keep These Points in Mind As You Brainstorm Your Knowledge Products:

- Students identify issues, frame arguments, and determine points that must be explored for evidence
- Students become content experts as they continue to probe
- Students see relationships in ideas, connections
- Students become experts and discover the questions central to the issue
- Students use rich information sources
- Students focus and structure research
- Students think deeply
- Students analyze and synthesize
- Students demonstrate deep knowledge
- Students transfer new knowledge to build broader understanding

Otherwise, You May Find Yourself Reverting Back to a Traditional Instructional Model:

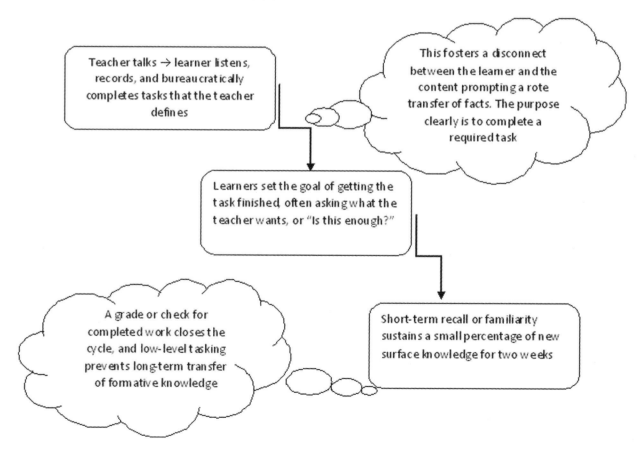

Teacher talks → learner listens, records, and bureaucratically completes tasks that the teacher defines

This fosters a disconnect between the learner and the content prompting a rote transfer of facts. The purpose clearly is to complete a required task

Learners set the goal of getting the task finished, often asking what the teacher wants, or "Is this enough?"

A grade or check for completed work closes the cycle, and low-level tasking prevents long-term transfer of formative knowledge

Short-term recall or familiarity sustains a small percentage of new surface knowledge for two weeks

EQ: How Does a Knowledge Product Differ from An Information Product? (*Continued*)

Information Product Design May Have These Low-Level Thought Characteristics:

- Partial or insufficient background knowledge
- Teachers often front load all prior knowledge
- Knowledge remains on a factual level
- Information seeking is seen as collecting facts
- Simple search strategies
- Squirreling, stockpiling, and Information overload
- Inability to reduce and manage information
- Shallow surface learning
- Relieved when the project is complete
- Low levels of interest and engagement
- Bureaucratically completing tasks (Zmuda)
- Missing relevant info
- High levels of insecurity
- Little evaluation, passive reception
- Reporting of mere facts found
- Technology "project" merely reporting facts without constructing meaning
- Predefined length
- Model that must be mirrored exactly with no room for creativity, innovation, or thinking outside the box
- Familiarity with previously done assignments

EQ: How Does Inquiry Shift
Roles for Learners and Teachers?

Inquiry learning shifts the roles of learners and of teachers in beneficial ways. Supported by brain-based research, these shifts optimize learning. Engagement, student-centered process, and higher-level thinking optimize learning outcome. Formative understanding of big ideas results from the manipulation, application, and use of information. Questioning, wonder, and curiosity spark a meaningful investigation by the learner. By connecting related facts, developing relevant big ideas, and generating a knowledge product, the learner moves beyond short-term recall to formative knowledge. That knowledge becomes the basis for new learning through the consolidation of ideas. Connections, relationships, and an expanding big picture of the world make sense!

Inquiry learning dynamics shift in four ways:

- Teacher directed to student centered
- Passive to active learner
- Rote to deep understanding
- Isolation to interaction

Edgar Dale points out that a passive learner, who is reading, listening, or tasking, will retain about 5% of what is learned two weeks later. Conversely, if a learner is engaged, developing meaningful questions for Inquiry, investigating multiple texts, socially interacting with peers, and actively creating and sharing a knowledge product, about 90% of what is learned is retained. A learner becomes a questioner, a decision maker. A learner constructs meaning, communicates, and shares. An active learner in Inquiry plans, thinks, devises strategies, validates, and reflects. An active learner in Inquiry owns the process and invests in the product. A trusting relationship with a teacher who coaches, guides, and encourages results in a student who cares and succeeds. Genuine empowerment occurs.

A common misconception regarding inquiry is that it sets learners loose to discover new knowledge on their own. Another embraces the belief that absent teacher-directed dynamics, chaos ensues. Neither is true. Guided Inquiry creates new roles for teachers that are highly effective. Research affirms that without guidance from the teacher, or a team of involved educators, learning does not take place. Time invested in unguided Inquiry produces misconceptions and frustration. Mastery level learners can benefit from less guidance after they have achieved a high degree of independence and skill. The diligent educator who scaffolds Inquiry learning experience, motivates, and differentiates optimizes outcomes. The teacher builds in guidance from the beginning to the end of Inquiry. However, the student is still the one who is doing the work and doing the learning.

EQ: How Does Inquiry Shift
Roles for Learners and Teachers? (*Continued*)

Teacher Roles in Inquiry:

- Generates curiosity, wonder
- Connects to prior knowledge
- Builds background knowledge
- Teaches the vocabulary of the discipline
- Prompts question development and brainstorming
- Provides framing questions and learning plan
- Builds understanding of important BIG IDEAS
- Frames the process and product, audience, purpose
- Encourages meaningful CHOICE

Then:

- Teaches target skills
- Continuously assesses for learning
- Designs activities and goals that are rigorous
- Confers with learners, listens
- Elicits evidence of progress
- Scaffolds and differentiates
- Manages access to information resources
- Teaches, models, and guides practice in literacy
- Provides feedback
- Teaches new skills
- Guides synthesis
- Insures opportunities to share knowledge products

A Sample Model

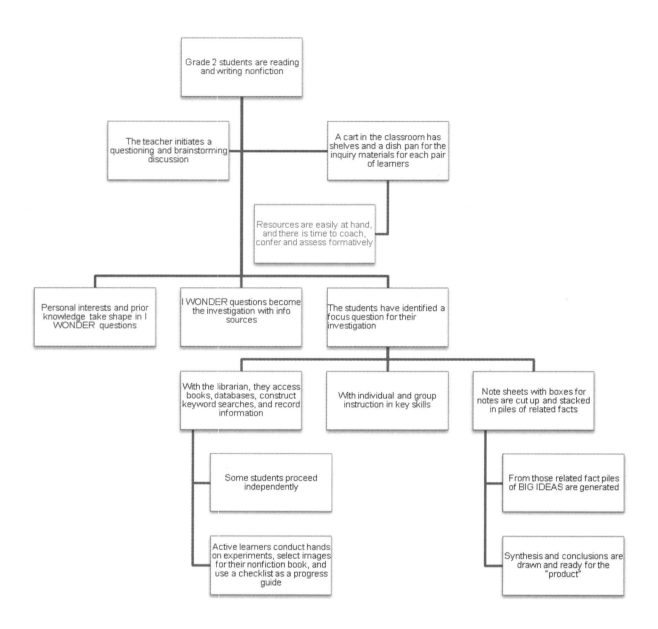

The class produces a writing project using technology such as PowerPoint, Storyboard, MuseumBox, etc. The computer lab aide may assist. The newly published nonfiction writing is featured in a hallway display or online. Enthusiastic students share their knowledge with engaged audiences. An iMovie is created of the kids speaking about their inquiry as toothless smiles abound, and reflection bubbles up.

Common Core Check

Consideration	√	Notes
How will we implement research projects based on multiple, complex, quality textual resources, insuring use of discipline specific vocabulary?		
How will we build background and integrate prior knowledge?		
How will we activate critical thinking, development of argument, questions?		
How will we insure synthesis of texts to generate evidence for argument?		
How will we reach the goal of deep understanding and content mastery?		
How are we using formative assessment to boost performance?		
How will we support collaboration and sharing using technology?		
How will we share our products with meaningful audiences?		

Frcm *Rx for the Common Core: Toolkit for Implementing Inquiry Learning* by Mary Boyd Ratzer and Paige Jaeger. Santa Barbara, CA: Libraries Unlimited. Copyright © 2014.

Common Core Building Blocks: Self-Check

How have you used the building blocks of the Common Core in your unit plan?

	How is the building block connected to the Common Core?	How is this building block connected to best practice/ APPR?	What are target student outcomes involving this building block?	What evidence of this building block is in your plan?
Questioning				
Synthesis				
Assessment				
Engagement				
Rigor/Depth of Knowledge				
Student-Centered Process				

4

Engagement

Being busy does not always mean real work. The object of all work is production or accomplishment and to either of these ends there must be forethought, system, planning, intelligence and honest purpose as well as perspiration. Seeming to do is not doing.

—Thomas A. Edison

EQ: How Do Teachers Engage Learners?

When spinning straw into gold, a magic word would come in handy. One of the most magical words of all in the classroom or school library is ENGAGE! For many years in one library, stood a life size, cardboard likeness of Captain Jean Luc Picard of the Star Ship *Enterprise*. Madness had not beset the librarian despite the occasional rumor. Quite the contrary, any Trekker could readily point out, Captain Picard's most identifiable punch line was just one word: "Engage!"

Engaging learners is actually well documented in theory, but sometimes bypassed in the quest for content or performance on tests. The grade two teacher, whose class betrays his disengagement after a stretch of testing, admits freely that his kids are "glassy eyed." A high school English teacher accounts for the quality of her day with the statement: "The heads were hitting the desks." Engaging a learner takes time and energy, but the payoff comes in the form of motivation, ownership, self-direction, stamina, shared ideas, and quality work. With the Common Core's emphasis on *active learners* and *content connections* to the real world, a gentle redirect brings us back to that magic word—ENGAGE!

Four fundamental, pedagogical shifts for initiating and sustaining engagement are:

- Shift from a teacher-centered to a learner-centered focus
- Encourage social interaction, personal response
- Build on authentic, real-world connections
- Insure meaningful choices

Four key decisions, in planning every unit plan, predict student engagement:

- Identifying compelling content (inherently engaging and relevant) that provides a rich and challenging landscape for new knowledge
- Eliciting prior knowledge of, and personal connections to, the content at hand
- Activating thinking with background building experiences, light up the content's BIG IDEAS of the discipline
- Committing to students sharing (or expressing) the summative knowledge product with an audience

I CARE. I COUNT. I CAN. Engagement is happening if a learner can express these brief reflections. Thinking in a BIG IDEA mindset is inherently engaging. Moving from lower-level thinking, to analysis, evaluation, and finally synthesis in an environment attuned to Inquiry is inherently engaging.

High-yield, instructional strategies, identified by Marzano and others, fuel active learning. Concept mapping, seeing relationships among facts, using information sources to solve problems, visual and graphical representation, generating and testing conclusions, and higher-level questions, are powerful separately and in combination.

Engagement's overarching truth is that the *learner needs a personal connection to the work at hand.* To be energized by learning, students need to be empathetic, connected in a community of learners, and collaborative. The learner needs to generate real-world products in this context and experience the lift of creativity. Interdisciplinary connections enhance the experience as well.

Analysis of engagement in the context of 21st-Century Skills, concluded that performance-based assessment further engaged learners as it demonstrated their success. Formative assessments such as graphic organizers, process guides, conferences with teachers, and peer reviews are examples of engaging innovative assessment models, which effectively engage learners.

Engagement Strategies Power Grid

Use this grid to self-assess the level of engagement in your Inquiry plan. Which characteristics are you using in your lessons? Highlight the boxes that are present in your instruction.

Big ideas	Personal choice	Meaning
CHOICE	VOICE	Responsibility
CONNECTIONS	Curiosity	Purpose
Collaboration	Originality	Generating hypotheses
Prior knowledge	Learner generated questions	**Real world**
Recognition	Authentic Tasks	FEEDBACK
CHALLENGE	Meaningful audience	TECHNOLOGY
BIG IDEAS	Learner centered	CRITICAL RESPONSE
Social interaction	COMMUNITY	CRITICAL THINKING
EMPATHY	Synthesis	Prior knowledge
Multidisciplinary	COMMUNICATE & SHARE	PRODUCE
Modeling	SUCCESS	Clear expectations

Engagement is a key expectation of the Danielson Framework for Professional Practice and the Common Core Learning Standards.

EQ: How Do You Foster Engagement and Student Ownership?

Front-loaders are great for carrying a load, moving a pile, and leveling ground. When you build a home, a front-loader is one of the first large machines used. The owners get all excited to see ground broken and their ownership dream begins to be realized. Inquiry-based learning follows the same pattern. If you cheat and skimp on the front-end, you will miss the transfer of excitement and ownership during the process.

The very act of allowing students to brainstorm, gather and list questions, wonder about details, link to prior knowledge, discuss, and metacognitively bathe in the topic—is the same process that transforms the assignment from teacher directed to student centered. As students are allowed to form the curriculum into something that is relevant to their "being," the assignment moves from being the teacher's to belonging to the student. Students will begin to use the first person "I" and "mine" when talking about their work. That's when you know you have been successful in transferring ownership.

A number of years ago, a noncollaborative social studies teacher arrived at the library for "research." At the end of the two days a sharp student named Shawn was leaving the library with his low-level fact regurgitation research on "Suffragettes" and deposited his paper in the trash on the way out. Turning he said, "I don't get it. Why do we have to learn about these women anyway? Are they suffering anymore?"

Shawn was right. To learn about independent, isolated women who looked miserable and old was not relevant to his world in any way. There was no front-end loading, there was no relevance fostered. He never got to the first person in suffragette. If he and his group had been able to front-load, they may have come up with questions such as:

- Who fostered this situation where women were not treated equal?'
- Where is "suffrage" still occurring in the world?
- Who else have we treated in this manner?
- How does the social climate that existed in the United States during the suffragette movement compare to Islamic nations with Sharia law?
- What are the parallels between the woman's rights movements and civil rights' movements?
- Are there any notable women in oppressive nations today that deserve to be recognized as these suffragettes were?
- How can I be inspired to stand up for something I believe in today?
- How does the Bill of Rights support my right to advocate for change?
- How can I be a change agent and what would I change?

EQ: How Do You Foster Engagement and Student Ownership? (*Continued*)

Note the difference in these questions compared to typical fact-based hunting questions on Susan B. Anthony. Note the "relevance" that is fostered when you allow the students to generate questions. The questions typically dig deeper to the real meaning of the content.

Letting go of the front-end is hard for teachers. This can be messy, but—it can be rewarding also.

Let your students activate their thinking! Let them get messy and wander in the subject matter. It is in the wandering that they pick up related core content vocabulary and begin to find pieces that they put together. You are their *learning concierge*. You can provide the metacognitive path of discovery. As you model the thought process, they will learn to think, investigate, synthesize, and create. They will uncover and discover.

EQ: Whatz up with da Gen Ys?

They've been called the *Me Generation*, the *Millennials, Gen Y*s, and more. They've been criticized, glamorized, proselytized, and capitalized. For all their faults, they show great potential—if we can tap their skills, creativity, and technological know-how for good uses.

Our students have been raised *inside,* connected, and have been influenced by the media more than any other generation on the face of the planet. They are device addicted, technologically dependent, metacognitively challenged, and socially deprived. When the Pew Internet studies announced that this generation exits school and "connects" at home for more than five hours a day, teachers fumed wondering why students could not get their homework done. They failed to see that their assignments need "repackaging." We favor Inquiry-based learning as the new recipe for success.

Inquiry works for the millennial generation because it transfers ownership to the learner. With the Inquiry model, the assignment is no longer the teacher's assignment, but the students' work. If you can get your students to the point where they are talking about "their" work, their topic, their product, or their world, then you have succeeded. Inquiry promotes the following dispositions to make your assignment a success:

- Student ownership
- Student engagement
- Student choice
- Student voice
- Authentic learning tasks
- Real-world applications
- Assignments completed

When assignments start with a question, the student has a destination—a purpose.

When assignments foster curiosity, the students will want answers.

When students are allowed an element of choice, they own the assignment.

When students are given the opportunity to voice their knowledge, they have direction and purpose.

This millennial generation is social, curious and research demonstrates that they want to change the world. They value experience and can be motivated by change, technology, and real-world answers. Therefore, as today's educators, we need to capitalize on these characteristics for academic success and Inquiry affords us this opportunity.

EQ: What Type of Sources Should Be "Allowed" for This Transliterate Generation?

This generation is called the transliterate generation because they are "reading" across media platforms. No longer are information and reading confined to black and white print. Literacy is now three dimensional, printed in color, archived in movie formats, discussed on blogs, read on billboards, and printed on old-fashioned paper. Students "kangaroo" from one website to the next, skimming, scanning, and assessing at warp speed. While some see this as an asset, the Common Core in Appendix A, page 4, paragraph 2 contends that these students need another skill in addition to the quick ability to squirrel away facts: They need to focus, examine, draw evidence from the text, properly giving attribution, and speak with authority.

While this transliterate generation might quickly find information, students need to take the next big step and examine their information for use and meaning. Students may need to be informed of or taught this new mode of operation. You can experiment with your elementary schools with a movement called *Inform and Transform.* Prior to computer research, we encourage students to slow down and realize they are not in an entertainment mode but are in an education mode.

The expectation is that by metacognitively pointing out that educational use of a screen, or computer, needs deeper focus and examination than they use for playing games, students will begin to distinguish between the two forms of computer use—entertainment and examination. This transliterate generation is not limited to one form of information, but rather is challenged to examine all sources for use, but they often have to slow down to do this.

This generation may be great at searching YouTube.com for a variety of transliterate appropriate sources, and can indeed find valuable information. We can help them examine the source and cite these sources if they add breadth to their information. *However,* as the Common Core states, these tweets, videos, podcasts may add value; but they cannot match the depth and difficulty that are needed to educate mathematicians, scientists, actuaries, lawyers, doctors, and other detail-oriented professionals that make us globally competitive.

The conclusion that many educators arrive at is to allow this transliterate generation to use a breadth of resources, but require additional, deeper, more difficult resources to be used to support research. This correlates with the Common Core expectations to draw evidence from the text, support positions, build arguments, examine and communicate, all the while avoiding plagiarism. When a student is expected to give attribution, as stated in the Common Core writing standard number 8, it is more likely that plagiarism will be avoided. Rubrics should reflect this requirement: "Student backs up claims with quotes." Rather than: "Works Cited attached."

EQ: What Part Does Technology Play in the Inquiry Model?

We live in a technology-infused world and we teach a classroom of technology-dependent students. To deliver instruction void of technology is to speak a different language. If you are tech-savvy, you are two steps ahead. Read on to insure that you are integrating technology for higher-level thought. If you are tech impaired, consider making a goal to learn and integrate one new tech tool monthly into your instruction and journal the difference this makes.

Research shows when you integrate technology into instruction, there is an increase in student achievement. However, this achievement is likely due to the fact the students are engaged and thus will score higher. Using the same logic, we can speculate that if technology is infused into a lesson with higher-level thought, student achievement will surpass those lessons without higher-level thought.

Time and time again teachers create "great projects" where technology has been infused, but the knowledge product appears as a simple information hide 'n seek report delivered with a technology ribbon. Educators should strive to use technology for communicating original conclusions, deep understanding, and new knowledge. Technology provides the vehicle for quality synthesized information.

- As we continue to unwrap the Inquiry model, strategically integrate technology throughout the Inquiry process.

Every year, the American Association of School Libraries identifies the 25 Best Technology Tools for Learning. These are often organized by the phases of Inquiry cycle. A simple Google search will land you on the correct page. Start there for technology ideas, if this is new for you.

Technology plays essential roles in the Inquiry cycle from activating thinking, investigating information, synthesizing meaning, collaborating, and wrapping up the knowledge product into a media-infused model.

If your school's technology is less-than-stellar, you can often replicate technology tools with older analog measures. One local teacher could not access "Stixy .com for student questioning and simply chose to post a large wall of bulletin board paper and let the students post their notes with markers. The result was the same—engagement.

5

Thinking and Questioning

The outcome of any serious research can only be to make two questions grow where only one grew before.

—Thorstein Veblen

EQ: How Are Questions at the Heart of Inquiry Learning and the Common Core?

Questions are at the heart of Inquiry learning. They generate wonder and engagement. Questions drive deep and authentic learning, uncovering meaning and connections. As the catalysts for synthesis and understanding they are powerful and essential. Questions open mental windows and doors to ideas, relevance, and insight.

Skilled use of higher-order questions by teachers and librarians lift the thinking of the learner to a level where multiple possibilities present themselves. With the capacity to guide learners in question development, teachers model question development. Concept mapping the brainstormed questions of young learners can capture the big ideas of a topic at hand. More importantly that map or KWL (Know, Want to know, Learned) chart connects the learner to the content dimensions through related questions, even unrelated questions.

Engaged and curious, the learner generates big questions, investigates, frames new questions, and continues in a cycle. Even the final phase of Inquiry, when a knowledge product has been shared with a meaningful audience, continues the flight with questions that still need to be pursued. The relevance of questions to the learning at hand often mines the dimensions of a discipline or curricular content. The sign on the classroom door should read "Lifelong learning in progress."

Investing time and thought to master questioning pays off in the rigor and relevance of student work, genuine assimilation of academic vocabulary, and quality of summative products. The rote report, where facts line up in a list, stays firmly grounded in who, what, where, and when. Short-term recall of discreet facts is all an educator can hope for in this kind of work. Moving questioning up the ladder of Bloom's Taxonomy determines a shift to long-term transfer of learning. At the level of synthesis, understanding that emerges becomes a permanent part of a mindscape of sorts. New learning consolidates and connects with prior big ideas and details. Interdisciplinary connections find a home base, integrating ideas that are related across contexts. The novice or apprentice thinker moves toward expertise.

Socratic questions, essential questions, guiding questions, and student-generated questions go hand-in-hand with practice and modeling for both teacher and learner. Transparent consideration of questions is ongoing in the Inquiry classroom. Many classrooms have incorporated a simple wonder wall, or wonder center, where questions can be posted. This can open the flood gates of curiosity for a young learner. Self-generated and deep questions can transform flat research tasks into meaningful and relevant pursuits for older learners. Resounding evidence supports the power of the question to give wings to those who find their way, and depart from one right answer.

EQ: What's the Scoop on Text-Dependent Questions?

There is a biblical proverb that says, "In all your getting, get understanding." If you ask students today what they would like to get, they would probably say, "rich" or "a new car" or "a place on the football team." Students usually do not equate *getting* with understanding. However, they often remark, "I just don't get it" when they do not understand.

The Common Core is asking teachers to create valuable questions—golden questions—which will lead students to understand a particular close reading passage. We are to create prospectors of our students so as they read, they mine for meaning. Text-dependent questions (TDQs) do just that.

Here's the Scoop on TDQs:

- TDQs specifically ask a question that can only be answered by referring back to the text.
- TDQs do not rely on prior knowledge or experiences.
- A TDQ requires students to spotlight something from their reading to answer it.
- A TDQ is a guide to understanding because in answering the question, the student will find meaning.
- A good TDQ will bring a student to important pieces of the passage and cause him or her to digest and conclude to find a golden nugget of meaning.
- A good TDQ will ask a reader to consider the use of specific words the author may have used precisely—in order to heighten awareness to vocabulary or depth of meaning.
- A good TDQ spotlights grammatical or sentence structure changes used to make a point, or build or reinforce ideas with writing style patterns.
- A good TDQ should not give away the answer or meaning but help students uncover or discover it.

With the Common Core taking a stand on "literacy across the disciplines" it is high time for school librarians to see themselves as instructional partners—as teachers—as those having an opportunity to impact student achievement. Librarians can ask TDQs when students are in the library. Good TDQs can easily be used for read alouds or to find meaning in research articles. These TDQs are almost the polar opposite of Inquiry-Based Questions.

When students closely read and examine a text, they should be given a set of TDQs that guide them to discover and understand the key ideas.

Below is a TDQ tool that may help to create quality TDQs for a read aloud, or close read that takes place before an Inquiry endeavor:

Look for	Ideas
What's the big message?	
What's the theme?	
Can I ask an easy question first to build confidence?	
Are there any arguments? Two sides?	
Are there any key vocabularies of the discipline that are critically placed for understanding?	
Are there any powerful academic vocabulary words that may have been used?	
How is the passage constructed and is it for a purpose?	
Identify the toughest part of the text and ask questions to help clarify meaning	
Order your questions to scaffold understanding of the passage overall	
The TASK: What can we ask the students to do with their knowledge? Discussion, debate, writing, further research? Ponder questions?	

Caveat: Most teachers have not learned how to create a set of TDQs yet. Librarians can serve as building leaders to model this recipe and roll this out to colleagues.

Librarians can participate in "literacy across the content areas" by creating TDQs for read aloud books. The Common Core Appendix A addresses read alouds as an opportunity to model fluency, but also as an important venue for metacognitive modeling. This is one way we can model supporting answers with evidence from the text.

Librarians can suggest that teachers plan a short research activity after a "close read" with TDQs, in order to get the students wondering and investigating beyond the text. This would require students to move from TDQs to Inquiry questions.

Inquiry-based questions require students to research beyond the text. TDQs are opposite in nature, where they require students to remain in the close reading text.

Using open-ended questions is a good way to lead a discussion after a close reading activity.

The Socractic Guide is followed by 99 Golden Nuggets—samples of Inquiry-based questions. Examine these questions and compare these Inquiry Essential Questions to research projects on similar topics that might be done in your school. Please note the open-endedness of these 99 questions and see how the student would have to investigate, synthesize, conclude, in order to find meaning from multiple texts.

The Socratic questioning technique is an effective way to explore ideas in depth. By *questioning,* teachers promote independent thinking and student ownership. Higher-level thinking skills are present while students think, discuss, debate, evaluate, and analyze.

Recently, R.W. Paul's six types of Socratic Questions were expanded to nine types. These questions are reproduced with permission from the Foundation for Critical Thinking. For a more complete description of Socratic Questioning, see *The Thinker's Guide to the Art of Socratic Questioning* (2007), by Richard Paul and Linda Elder. Details may be found at www.criticalthinking.org.

Further Questions for Socratic Dialogue

Questions of Clarification

- What do you mean by _____?
- What is your main point?
- How does _____ relate to _____?
- Could you put that another way?
- What do you think is the main issue here?
- Is your basic point _____ or _____?
- Could you give me an example?
- Would this be an example: _____?
- Could you explain that further?
- Would you say more about that?
- Why do you say that?
- Let me see if I understand you; do you mean _____ or _____?
- How does this relate to our discussion/problem/issue?
- What do you think John meant by his remark? What did you take John to mean?
- Jane, would you summarize in your own words what Richard has said?
- Richard, is that what you meant?

Questions That Probe Purpose

- What is the purpose of _____?
- What was your purpose when you said _____?
- How do the purposes of these two people vary?
- How do the purposes of these two groups vary?
- What is the purpose of the main character in this story?
- How did the purpose of this character change during the story?
- Was this purpose justifiable?
- What is the purpose of addressing this question at this time?

Questions That Probe Assumptions

- What are you assuming?
- What is Karen assuming?
- What could we assume instead?
- You seem to be assuming _____. Do I understand you correctly?

- All of your reasoning depends on the idea that _____. Why have you based your reasoning on _____ rather than _____?
- You seem to be assuming _____. How would you justify taking this for granted?
- Is it always the case? Why do you think the assumption holds here?

Questions That Probe Information, Reasons, Evidence, and Causes

- What would be an example?
- How do you know?
- What are your reasons for saying that?
- Why did you say that?
- What other information do we need to know before we can address this question?
- Why do you think that is true?
- Could you explain your reasons to us?
- What led you to that belief?
- Is this good evidence for believing that?
- Do you have any evidence to support your assertion?
- Are those reasons adequate?
- How does that information apply to this case?
- Is there reason to doubt that evidence?
- What difference does that make?
- Who is in a position to know if that is the case?
- What would convince you otherwise?
- What would you say to someone who said _____?
- What accounts for _____?
- What do you think is the cause?
- How did this come about?
- By what reasoning did you come to that conclusion?
- How could we go about finding out whether that is true?
- Can someone else give evidence to support that response?

Questions about Viewpoints or Perspectives

- You seem to be approaching this issue from _____ perspective. Why have you chosen this rather than that perspective?
- How would other groups/types of people respond? Why? What would influence them?
- How could you answer the objection that _____ would make?
- Can/did anyone see this another way?
- What would someone who disagrees say?
- What is an alternative?
- How are Ken's and Roxanne's ideas alike? Different?

Questions That Probe Implications and Consequences

- What are you implying by that?
- When you say _____, are you implying _____?

- But if that happened, what else would also happen as a result? Why?
- What effect would that have?
- Would that necessarily happen or only probably happen?
- What is an alternative?
- If this and this are the case, then what else must be true?

Questions about the Question

- How can we find out?
- Is this the same issue as _____?
- How could someone settle this question?
- Can we break this question down at all?
- Is the question clear? Do we understand it?
- How would _____ put the issue?
- Is this question easy or difficult to answer? Why?
- What does this question assume?
- Would _____ put the question differently?
- Why is this question important?
- Does this question ask us to evaluate something?
- Do we need facts to answer this?
- Do we all agree that this is the question?
- To answer this question, what other questions would we have to answer first?
- I'm not sure I understand how you are interpreting the main question at issue.

Questions That Probe Concepts

- What is the main idea we are dealing with?
- Why/how is this idea important?
- Do these two ideas conflict? If so, how?
- What was the main idea guiding the thinking of the character in this story?
- How is this idea guiding our thinking as we try to reason through this issue? Is this idea causing us problems?
- What main theories do we need to consider in figuring out _____?
- Are you using this term "_____" in keeping with educated usage?
- What main distinctions should we draw in reasoning through this problem?
- What idea is this author using in her or his thinking? Is there a problem with it?

Questions That Probe Inferences and Interpretations

- What conclusions are we coming to about _____?
- On what information are we basing this conclusion?
- Is there a more logical inference we might make in this situation?
- How are you interpreting her behavior? Is there another possible interpretation?
- What do you think of _____?
- How did you reach that conclusion?
- Given all the facts, what is the best possible conclusion?
- How shall we interpret these data?

GOLD MINE OF 99 ESSENTIAL QUESTIONS FROM THE REAL WORLD!

1. How big is your carbon footprint?

2. How would you win and use a million dollar grant to reduce CO_2 emissions in a country of your choice?

3. Why do you need to be concerned about plate tectonics and the plate that is under your feet?

4. How does where you live determine how you live?

5. Why is individual empathy an engine for the health of a democracy?

6. What does it mean to have or not to have a home?

7. How could you convince a person to come to the new world from the old world?

8. How do geopolitical factors contribute greatly to the collapse of civilizations?

9. How do I affect the environment around me through personal choice?

10. Why did historically only 4% of the world's population live in a democracy?

11. How is health and wellness defined by the technology of the time?

12. How does the movement of people around the world influence the global community?

13. Why do humans need insects?

14. How would you pack your suitcase to visit Florida and Alaska?

15. How do animals think like scientists?

16. Why was Columbus a hero or a villain?

17. How was man the measure of all things in the Renaissance?

18. Why does America need to better respond to the tangible and intangible baggage of war?

19. How did the Universal Declaration of Human Rights expand the world's view of fundamental rights?

20. How was *Jane Eyre* by Charlotte Bronte a catalyst for social reform?

21. How can 21st-century New Yorkers improve their lives by adopting ideas from the Iroquois?

22. Why is your digital footprint a real-world character reference?

23. How do constructive and destructive forces change the world we live in?

24. How do you transform a dystopia to a utopia?

25. How does tragedy influence change?

26. How does the literature of Steinbeck reveal the pursuit of an American Dream?

27. How can humans mimic successful animals and their adaptations?

28. How can mathematical proportions provide evidence for improving zoo habitats?

29. How does Harry Potter employ renaissance medicine?

30. How was everyday life in Colonial times different from everyday life today?

31. How do companies and organizations improve conditions for people and the planet by corporate giving?

32. Why are endangered animals endangered?

33. How can statistics lie?

34. How is the U.S. justice system biased?

35. Why could Abraham Lincoln be impeached?

36. How can writing about negative experiences and circumstances actually help others?

37. How do slave narratives generate convictions regarding human rights?

38. How do nutrition and physical activity affect health?

39. Why is the U.S. Constitution an ideal form of government?

40. How can we write and abide by a classroom constitution?

41. How did the actions and beliefs of individuals save the Union from 1861 to 1865?

42. How does social responsibility sell?

43. How can statistics, data, and analysis of graphical information predict outcomes of lifestyle choices?

44. How do body systems support life?

45. How does the Hudson River tell the history of New York?

46. Why is showing respect to all individuals important?

47. How does geography affect the intensity and outcomes of natural disasters?

48. How do communities reflect how people work and play?

49. How can we determine when technological advances become harmful?

50. How should guidelines for advancing technology be decided?

51. What would the world be like without tone, tempo, and creativity?

52. How can technology make us smarter, richer, and more successful?

53. How does point of view affect opinion, bias, and advertising?

54. How could you use linguistic and cultural knowledge to survive if you woke up in a foreign country alone?

55. How do those who live in the Blue Zone provide a path to health and long life?

56. Why did immigrants face the unknown for the hope of a better life?

57. How does adaptation of animals differ by environment?

58. How can a high-school senior advocate for economic policy that will positively affect their personal economy in the next 10 years?

59. Why and how is the human experience connected across time, culture, and place?

60. How is the social gospel of the Gilded Age relevant for the rich and poor in America today?

61. How can you overcome personal obstacles and hardship in order to achieve a balanced and successful life?

62. How can an individual's actions change wrong to right?

63. Why is a specific storm the most difficult to survive?

64. How can the significant regional problems and promise of states drive change that benefits the United States?

65. How do I become an agent of change?

66. Why is guilt or innocence sometimes not absolute?

67. How do the actions of leaders distinguish them despite risk, challenge, and opposition?

68. Did explorers change the world for the better or the worse?

69. Why do living things change over time?

70. How would King George and a colonist have opposing viewpoints regarding the Boston Tea Party?

71. How do Dark Ages begin and end?

72. Why is my community important and how does it help me?

73. How does my community respond to wants and needs with goods and services?

74. How do ideas, values, and beliefs shape and unify American culture?

75. How do ideas, values, and beliefs change over time and fracture American culture?

76. How was nationalism born out of the colonial experience?

77. How did the colonies achieve independence from Great Britain?

78. Why were the Articles of Confederation insufficient for governing the new United States?

79. How do people emerge as strong leaders at times of unrest?

80. How does lack of freedom lead to revolution?

81. How does the journey impact the destination in a biography or memoir?

82. How did the reconstruction amendments lead to the civil rights movement?

83. How did Jim Crow cause the South to revert to a pre-Civil War society?

84. How is the culture of foreign country different from American culture, and why?

85. How do the mechanics of a musical instrument affect its sound?

86. How do the geographical features of the Adirondacks influence people's lives in our region?

87. How do the arts reflect what is happening in a time and place?

88. How do the collages of Romare Bearden and the work of other Harlem Renaissance artists express themes shared by poets and musicians of the time?

89. Why is the understanding of ionic and covalent and metallic bonding critical in the development of new products and technologies?

90. How do living things use their senses to adapt to the world around them?

91. How does pond life use a specialized habitat to survive and reproduce?

92. How does human decision making impact living things in our community?

93. How could smoking one pack of cigarettes a day affect a person each month?

94. How can we influence our government to protect citizens from the dangers of tobacco?

95. How would the world be different if we spend five minutes a week advocating for something we believe in?

96. Why did the Treaty of Versailles cause World War II?

97. How does autocracy impact individuals economically, socially, politically, and culturally?

98. How does the growth of plants in a garden relate to varying conditions?

99. How can slope inform decisions about outdoor sports and activities?

Prescription for Assessing Thinking: A Research CAPSULE

College and career readiness is fundamentally linked to healthy critical thinking. Evidence of critical thinking can be documented in what learners say, write, and express. When we encourage learners to think out loud, we can diagnose a thinking level and incubate an environment where thinking is valued and improved. Thinking is a strong factor in learning success. As teachers we should strive to strengthen these habits of mind through Inquiry learning in order to produce life-long thinkers. Teachers can prompt thinking with higher-level questions by modeling quality thinking and by using Socratic questioning techniques. Research improves thinking quality. Assessing thinking while teaching can be done with a range of thinking rubrics. Harvard's Artful Thinking website, called *Thinking in Mind,* and the Intel website offer straightforward criteria for the quality of thinking. The scale given here provides a composite of thinking levels as a first step in establishing usable gradients.

Thinking starting point	Thinking target
Surface only, based on familiarity, basic information, or on misinformation	Evidence of applications, connections, analysis
Confusion and inaccuracy regarding a key problem or issue, no attention to data	Problem clearly stated with consideration for related ideas, subtle but important points, data
Proceeds from a single perspective or inaccurate perspective	Proceeds from multiple, salient perspectives based on diverse information sources
Ignores underlying assumptions	Questions assumptions and ideas that are inherently related to an issue, verifies
Disregards the point of view of information or opinion	Analyzes the point of view of information or opinion, its underlying purpose, and validity
Restates facts without drawing general conclusions using the facts	Draws conclusions supported by concepts, evidence, relevant information
Skims information and records available facts	Synthesizes relevant information from multiple texts to support conclusions
Questions limited to who, what, where, when	Develops relevant, complex questions to clarify, extend, and widen issues

Tishman, Shari. "Assessing Thinking: Six Continua" (Chart developed for the Artful Thinking Project, Project Zero, Harvard Graduate School of Education). *Project Zero Website,* May 9, 2013. http://www.old-pz.gse.harvard.edu/tc/content/assessment/6Continua.pdf.

EQ: How Do Student Actions Produce Depth of Knowledge and Rigor?

The significance and dimensions of *depth* are elusive for the hyperconnected youth who operates in tweets and data bytes. Rather than asking probing questions about issues, problems, and events, these learners resort to chatter rife with the words "like," "lots," "really," "stuff," and "ya know?" The Common Core asks educator to triage the thinking power of learners who have grown up operating a mile wide and an inch deep. The thinking switch needs to turn from dim to penetrating.

When learners engage in Inquiry, they have an opportunity to demonstrate depth of knowledge and cognitive rigor in their actions, knowledge products, and dispositions. Evidence of rigorous thinking, speaking, and writing begins when the learner moves beyond the text. When learners are asked to connect concepts or ideas, generalize, or reason they are crossing the thinking bridge to depth and rigor. They will leave behind recall and rote as they infer, analyze, and conclude. Themes, issues, and problems are ideal for Inquiry.

Depth of knowledge is achieved when learners read multiple texts, discerning perspectives, validity, gaps, facts, and opinions. Addressing the overarching theme or issue in multiple complex texts demonstrates cognitive rigor. Extended thinking generates a sense of relationships between new and prior knowledge and often leads to the use of successful strategies for learning that have worked in other contexts. Working with conceptual frameworks and essential questions, teachers lift learners into higher-level thought.

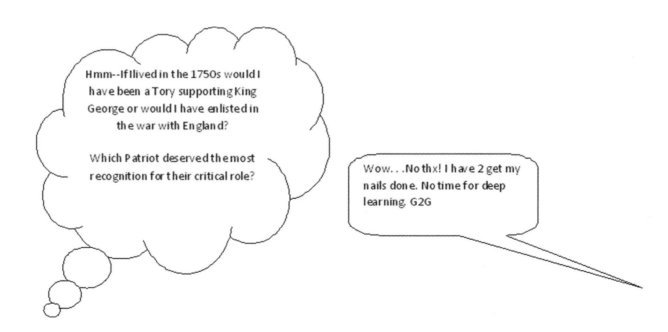

EQ: How Do Student Actions Produce Depth of Knowledge and Rigor? (*Continued*)

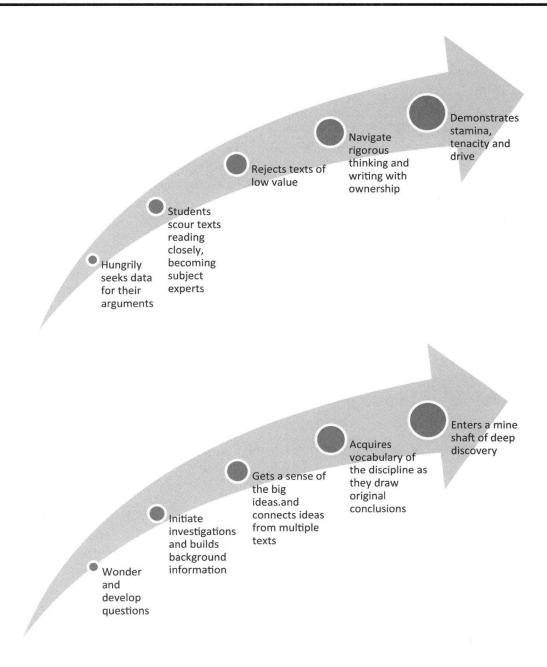

In contrast, students tasked with research click and pick, bounce in and out of texts with no authentic purpose. They get stuck when they don't find answers and grind to a disenfranchised halt. Disengaged students plug in whatever comes along on Google.

EQ: Is There a Remedy
for Low-Level Thought?

In the old research model, students had to be taught how and where to find information. Information is now found in our pockets. This hyperconnected generation has no trouble finding information—they just are unaware of how little the information they find is of bona fide use. A few students may stop to examine whether the website looks credible, but do they dig deeper to examine the authority of the Web address?

When we were young, the nightly business news consisted of the *who, what, when, where, and how.* Seldom did we hear the "why" of a news report, and if we did it was always preceded with a disclaimer from the station manager's warning, *"The commentary you are about to hear does not represent the views of this station or the . . . blah, blah, blah."* The news has evolved into commentary that reflects political views and often these views *do* reflect the values of the station and the station managers. Bias is rampant as we live in a fiercely divided political country. This is most often transparent to our students. The need now is not how to find information, but rather how to discern whether information is usable, valid, or biased. We should have an AUP—acceptable use policy—for information as well as technology.

In old research models, students were given 10 or 20 questions to research on a topic. These models are a travesty in today's Information Age. Most of these "questions" are answered via a simple Google search and are void of higher-level thought. In a true Inquiry model, the students are generating questions (as we have discussed in the *Wonder* phase previously). With these student-generated questions, students should be taught to dig deep, examine, evaluate, and mine for meaning.

> *Litmus test for higher-level thought: If your assignment is answerable on Google, it is void of higher-level thought. Throw it out.*

Librarians are now needed more than ever, but for a different reason. During the investigation stage, students now need to learn how to assess the credibility, accuracy, reliability, and support of gathered information. Librarians can guide students to credible, vetted databases that have aggregated information from credible sources. Librarians will help you teach information literacy to this information illiterate generation. Just because a teacher knows how to cook, does not mean they would bring a class to the Home and Careers classroom to bake a cake. Under the same logic we can claim: just because a teacher can access information does not mean they would bring their class to the library and instruct them how to find information. A librarian should be consulted as to the best avenue for information retrieval.

In the old print paradigm there were editors and gatekeepers of information. When a book was published, you could trust that the company had risked their reputation on insuring that the contents were vetted, appropriate, and correct. On the Internet, there is no longer this degree of confidence. More than ever, we must adopt a policy to scrutinize all websites to approve their use for investigation and research. Websites are not innocent until proven guilty. They are guilty until proven innocent.

EQ: Do Students Have to Worry about Bias and Inaccurate Information?

The Common Core Learning Standards expect learners to discern multiple perspectives, the credibility of perspectives, and the contrast of fact and opinion. Knowledge and sound thinking about an area under investigation are required of the student researcher. Assessing information resources includes skillful analysis of text for bias.

The following checklist guides the critical reader in identifying and responding to bias in information.

Critical Readers:

- Compare multiple texts from a variety of sources
- Look for word choices that convey bias, especially when comparing multiple texts on the same topic
- Be alert for information that is omitted, not verified, anonymous, or partial
- Recognize slant when context changes how facts are presented or emphasized
- Note the sources that contribute to a piece of text, authority of those sources, and possible affiliation with organizations or groups with special interests
- Go beyond a one-sided approach to the topic that overlooks or dismisses opposing views
- Evaluate texts for unfavorable headlines, photographs, captions, word choices, TV narration, and stereotypes
- Avoid texts that label and use titles for people, places, and events
- Check for a credible author, his expertise, his purpose, his qualifications, relationship to the topic, and status in his field
- Consider the date of the text and the relationship of the publication date to the big picture of the topic
- Evaluate the basic nature of the text: objective study, an opinion piece, informational, persuasive
- Be aware of the publisher or Web URL and judge objectivity, potential for economic or political gain, and alignment with one perspective
- Avoid text that incorporates error, misinformation, or stereotypes

We are living in an age where information on the Internet almost has to be "assumed guilty" and credibility evaluated prior to any use. Misinformation and biased and erroneous information probably exceed valid information.

Higher-Level Thinking, Questions, and Products

Level	Verbs	Products	Questions
Synthesizing	Build, create, design, develop, devise, generate, hypothesize, invent, propose, theorize, compose, construct, invent, improve, adapt, imagine, formulate	A model program to address social issue; inventing a new animal; creating a new country; designing a building, machine, process, experiment; developing legislation; devising an ethical code, a way to test a new concept or theory; creating a play, a song, a movie	What if? Why? How? Should? So what?
Transforming	Blend, build, combine, compile, conclude, compose, convince, decide, dramatize, express, forecast, imagine, modify, revise	Ad campaign, a board game, a poem or short story, a play, dialog, speech, role play, news show, historical newspaper, Web page	What is your: Conclusion? Connection? Prediction?
Challenging	Appraise, argue, assess, criticize, compare, debate, defend, judge, justify, rank, prioritize, refute, review, support, value, weigh, verify, recommend	Critical review, argue as an attorney, determine the worth of a project, defend a judgment, debate issues, evaluate information, investigate a problem, justify a rank	Which is better? How would you rate? refute? What evidence supports?
Analyzing	Analyze, apply, associate, break down, differentiate, change, compare, contrast, distinguish, examine, infer, experiment, relate, select, map, sift, solve	Create a timeline or flowchart and correlate events, transplant an event or person, write an obituary or review, letter to the editor, rewrite w/ new perspective, graphic	Why do you think? What justifies? How is this related? How can you distinguish?

(Continued)

Based on the *REACTS Taxonomy* by Barbara Stripling and Judy Pitts and *Bloom's Taxonomy*. From *Rx for the Common Core: Toolkit for Implementing Inquiry Learning* by Mary Boyd Ratzer and Paige Jaeger. Santa Barbara, CA: Libraries Unlimited. Copyright © 2014.

Higher-Level Thinking,
Questions, and Products (*Continued*)

Level	Verbs	Products	Questions
Explaining	Cite, complete, describe, document, explain, expand, give examples, illustrate, restate, paraphrase, generalize, show, solve, use, portray	Dramatize, illustrate, present a news show, fictional diary or narrative, resume for a person researched, explorer's log, journal, guided tour	What? Who? Where? When? What is different, the same?
Recalling	Arrange, cluster, find, identify, label, list, locate, match, name, recall, reproduce, select, state, recount	Select or list, find facts, select pictures, state questions of a reporter, arrange words, define words, write a letter recounting, chart facts, make a timeline	Who? What? Where? When?

RX FOR THE COMMON CORE: RESEARCH CAPSULE FOR QUESTIONING

A real world moment:

A visitor was sitting next to a student in a social studies classroom, where a lecture was in progress on Jacksonian democracy. The lecture was interspersed with numerous, high-volume rhetorical questions. The student noticed that the visitor surveyed the room for students ready to answer the questions. Turning to the visitor, the student politely provided advice: "At first we thought she wanted us to answer. But she really doesn't. That's just the way she talks."

—Mary Ratzer

Questioning is at the heart of Inquiry. Questioning is also an essential for delivery of the Common Core, in the classroom or library. As the catalyst for authentic investigation using multiple information sources, it is the engine for writing from sources and short and sustained research. Building meaning from text requires skilled questioning by teachers and learners. Depth of understanding cannot occur without it. Rigor and relevance evolve through higher levels of questioning.

See Appendix for Questioning charts and teaching aids.

Moving from surface facts to depth of understanding is the focus of the graphical representations. In each case, educational research and experience regarding questioning informs the ideas presented in charts, lists, and prompts. Concise, direct, visually enhanced, these graphical pages distill teaching strategies for the Common Core.

See Appendix for the WISE Guide to Questioning, Synthesis, and Assessment

6

Synthesis

Celebrate the understood, not the found.

—Ross Todd

EQ: Why Synthesize?

Synthesis gets top billing in Bloom's Taxonomy. The Common Core Learning Standards (for reading, writing, speaking, and listening) culminate in synthesis. There are many reasons why synthesis is the king of the learning hill. Essentially, the level of questioning, thinking, reading, and communication that occurs in synthesis builds new knowledge that lasts. Synthesis helps the novice mind build an ever expanding, big picture of the world. Synthesis leads to content mastery and hard wires key ideas.

During the often creative experience of synthesis, learners find their own voices, intrinsic motivation, and new questions to pursue. In contrast, the karaoke kid who restates found facts, mindlessly mouths the words to complete a task assigned. Those inert, disconnected facts are soon forgotten. As Ross Todd states, "Celebrate the understood, not the found."

Synthesis is essential to deep understanding. It begins with unrelated facts, and ends with complex connections that shape strong arguments and original ideas. The rigor of building meaning from texts, and drawing new conclusions, is a power pack for the mind and builds lifelong learning skills.

The Common Core sets a standard for multiple perspectives, critical engagement, and arguments forged with evidence to harness the power of synthesis. Studies in the Chicago City Schools and the Province of Ontario demonstrate the power of authentic intellectual work. A shift to rigor in models that require synthesis yield academic improvements for all learners.

Making work harder, not easier, is not just about the 21st-century work force. Challenging learners to analyze multiple texts, identify relationships among facts, interrogate opinions, make meaningful connections, and refine questions will result in increased achievement and personal understanding.

EQ: How Can I Foster Synthesis?

Before a learner spins the straw of unrelated facts into the gold of new knowledge, a rigorous and relevant cognitive endeavor is undertaken. The youngest child can wonder, investigate, synthesize, and express. Conclusions can be reached through questioning, observation, charting of data, concept mapping, and use of relevant information.

Prerequisites for drawing original conclusions from quality information resources include:

- Probing questions
- Strategic reading
- Thoughtful consideration of many perspectives

Probing Questions

How do animals use their sensory organs to survive in their habitat? How do communities support their members' wants and needs with goods and services? Why does the rainforest need to be saved for one of its indigenous species? How do constructive and destructive forces impact the world around us? How did a traveler on the Underground Railroad experience the best and worst of a bitter era? Why does ratio and proportion influence gardens? Answers to essential questions such as these cannot be found without synthesis.

Strategic Reading

Steps to synthesis for young learners begin with unrelated facts from multiple texts. Connecting those unrelated facts to a unifying main idea initiates the development of big ideas. Ultimately, a child remembers and builds on the conceptual framework of a content area. Meaningful details and core vocabulary are knowingly tied to the broader understanding. They are manipulated, used, and applied in shared knowledge products. At the level of synthesis, learners transfer their knowledge to new content areas, weaving as it were a neural net to figure out the world.

Many Perspectives

Older learners synthesize with the power of abstract, conceptual thinking. Critical engagement with peers and access to complex texts enhance the process of synthesizing. A thoughtful encounter with multiple perspectives and contradictory voices is a catalyst for decision making. Weak and strong arguments, false and valid assumptions are categorized. Meaning constructed with relevant information requires ongoing analysis and evaluation. Each fact is considered in the light of its own validity, and in its relationship to other facts. Patterns emerge. Self-assessment and formative assessment guide the learner to the most important new ideas. Separate elements are fused to form a coherent whole.

EQ: How Can I Foster Synthesis? (*Continued*)

Synthesis Is Evidenced When

- Christopher Columbus is put on trial as a hero or a villain
- Evidence is collected for an underlying common ground of witch hunts, Dark Ages, or holocausts throughout history that helps make sense of otherwise disconnected historical events
- Insight is generated to literary catalysts of social reform such as Dickens or Bronte or Sinclair Lewis, and learners get down to the *moral of the story*
- Complex thinking is used to weigh ethical considerations, or underlying scientific or technological progress
- Data is used to justify conclusions

At the heart of synthesis is the inherent reward of personal efficacy. The Karaoke Kids will know why the material is important, why they should care, and why it is worth their time. Creating and sharing an original knowledge product motivates and rewards with success, originality, relationships, purpose, and meaning—proving that synthesis has occurred.

I make haste.
I copy and paste.
I am the Karaoke Kid.
I got an A, and Mom says "Hooray!"
But the point is really missed.
All I did was look on the Net. "
It was stupid, disconnected and dry.
If I knew why, perhaps I would try.
But this is a waste, so I'll copy and paste.
I am the Karaoke Kid.

With my rote little facts, the task I attacked.
Indeed, I am the Synthesizer.
It made sense to explore the facts and much more.
to draw conclusions and prepare for debate.
So, when I'm employed and a big wage I generate,
They'll ask me to justify, argue and validate.
I'm college and career ready.
My progress has been steady as I mine for meaning and more.
For rote I do not have to apologize.
I have learned to Synthesize.

EQ: How Can I Foster Synthesis in Assignments?

Teddy was a challenged student and a sincerely great teen who played guitar like a professional. When he handed in his biography report of Andrea Sigovia we knew that a few paragraphs did not reflect his vocabulary and extended beyond his current operating linguistics. The music teacher approached Eddy about his act of plagiarism and he simply stated, "I copied it from the Internet. You didn't require me to think about it, just report it."

In his simplicity, he was profoundly correct. In our copy and paste world, educators often require very little beyond the copy-paste model. So, the question is *how can we get students to think about the information and transform the data into something personally relevant, meaningful and rigorous?* This requires synthesis.

- Synthesis in research is a little requirement with a big effect.
- Synthesis is the act of discovering that a pile of facts can produce meaning.
- Synthesis is the key to long-term retention.
- Synthesis is the difference between regurgitation of facts and imbedding meaning.
- Synthesis is the process of packaging information into a knowledge product that discusses the issue or concept, rather than the facts.
- Synthesis is the glue that holds facts together in a meaningful way.

This tech-savvy generation can access anything, but they cannot analyze and they cannot synthesize. This may be our fault. For years education has concentrated on leaving no child behind and we have focused on coverage and recall. It is high time to eliminate the low-level rote and recall research models and deliver content through this Inquiry model. The Inquiry model requires students to uncover, discover, and demonstrate meaning.

The Chicago City schools increased their test results by making five simple changes:

1. Make work harder, not easier
2. Connect all learning to the kids' real world
3. Emphasize metacognitive strategies
4. Formatively assess
5. Engage in research using multiple resources and social interactions

They required students to manipulate their random facts and create meaning. They started to play with concepts and issues. When something has meaning, it innately has value. When something has value, it will move into the child's long-term memory, thus increasing test scores. We take our hats off to Chicago as this parallels Inquiry-based learning models.

EQ: How Can I Foster Synthesis in Assignments? (*Continued*)

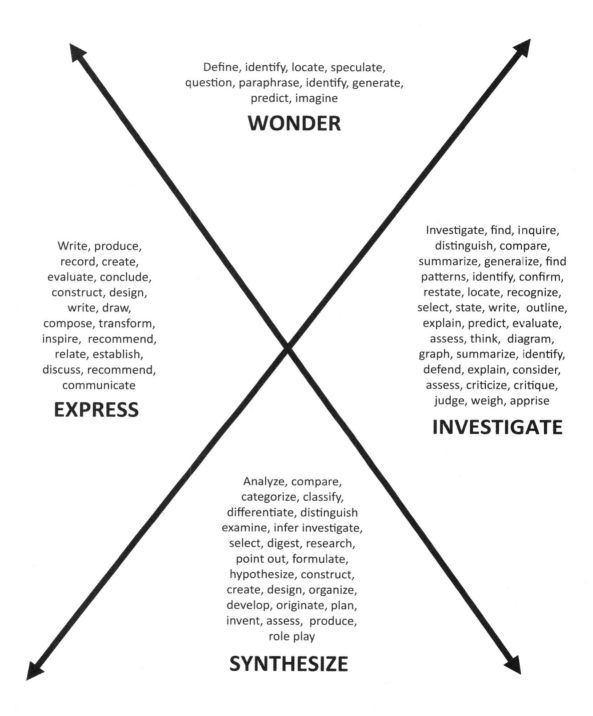

Define, identify, locate, speculate, question, paraphrase, identify, generate, predict, imagine

WONDER

Write, produce, record, create, evaluate, conclude, construct, design, write, draw, compose, transform, inspire, recommend, relate, establish, discuss, recommend, communicate

EXPRESS

Investigate, find, inquire, distinguish, compare, summarize, generalize, find patterns, identify, confirm, restate, locate, recognize, select, state, write, outline, explain, predict, evaluate, assess, think, diagram, graph, summarize, identify, defend, explain, consider, assess, criticize, critique, judge, weigh, apprise

INVESTIGATE

Analyze, compare, categorize, classify, differentiate, distinguish examine, infer investigate, select, digest, research, point out, formulate, hypothesize, construct, create, design, organize, develop, originate, plan, invent, assess, produce, role play

SYNTHESIZE

From *Rx for the Common Core: Toolkit for Implementing Inquiry Learning* by Mary Boyd Ratzer and Paige Jaeger. Santa Barbara, CA: Libraries Unlimited. Copyright © 2014.

EQ: How Can We Get Students to Filter the Valuable from Trivia?

An important skill for learners who are synthesizing related facts into big ideas is the sorting of useful information from useless information. The natural inclination of kids to act like squirrels and gather, stockpile, and consume whatever edibles might be lying around doesn't work in disciplined Inquiry. This practical target tool, used with intermediate learners, helps kids to see the distinction between trivia and super significant information. Simply have students take notes as usual. Then, ask them to color the target four different colors—with one color representing each layer of importance from vital to trivia. Ask students to color their notes and designate them according to the target scale. Final products will be constructed from only the two center areas, greatly upgrading their work in terms of relevance and strength.

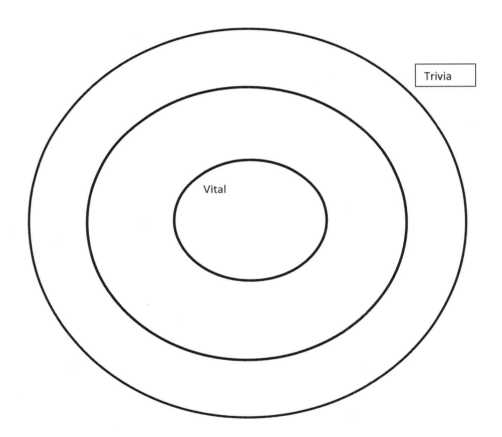

After students have sorted the valuable from the trivia, they may also have trouble synthesizing the most important information. At this point, a teacher can guide the process of mining for meaning by encouraging connections and relationships between facts. Examine the following lists for practical ideas. (This graphic may also be found in the Appendix.)

Analyze information for:
· Cause and effect
· Conclusions
· Categories
· Relationships
· Patterns
· Hierarchies
· Relevance
· Irrelevance
· Value
· Comparisons
· Contrasts
· Key concept
· Bias

Ask questions as you read:
· How is this organized?
· Can I map or outline this?
· Do I agree or disagree?
· What supports this point?
· What evidence is needed to prove this?
· Who would disagree with this?
· What information is needed to proceed?
· What is the point of view?
· How does this relate to other facts, data, or evidence I have?
· How important is this?

EQ: Why Is Synthesis Important, Anyway?

Shenedehowa High School in upstate New York featured an elective English program for juniors and seniors. One course drew in many seniors, focusing on Irish Literature and history. Students returning from Vocation and Technical (vo-tech) training, having just invested much energy in learning that was very relevant and experiential often populated the last class of the day. A thesis-based research project was a requirement of every senior, which included a white paper platform. Often more creative products spun off the rigorous paper.

Jim arrived from the bus with his predictably sideways hat. As the librarian supporting the thesis development, I asked him how his research was going. Jim was expected to read multiple sources, identify important main ideas, and synthesize these into a thesis and he was in process.

His response was, "Yeah, well, I'm doing pretty well. I am really thinking that the famine was a terrible thing. Did you know that a million and a half people died? Those potatoes got this blight from Holland, and they were poison if you ate them. They only grew potatoes, because this was a single crop economy. You know? I have been reading about the British and that Land Act of 1839. Did you know that they passed this law that no Irish could own land and that they had to grow potatoes for the landowners who were British? Did you know they did very little to help the starving people who got evicted when their crops failed?"

Jim's thesis was obvious, if unstated. A little prompt to get the thesis born resulted in this: "So, I'm thinking that the British were responsible for the deaths of a million and a half Irish during the Great Hunger."

Now that is a Common Core argument, with evidence, ready to be written. That is synthesizing the "facts" to form an opinion or position. That is drawing evidence from the text and citing sources. Without Synthesis, a project is copy–paste and not worth the doing. After all, facts can be looked up on a device at any time. Our objective is not to look up facts, but to infuse meaning and higher-level thought.

- It is synthesis that gives facts meaning
- It is in synthesis that a student makes "sense" of facts found
- It is in synthesis that we teach thought
- It is in synthesis that students feel empowered
- It is synthesis that lends an opportunity of creativity, insight, and application of "differences" that students have within themselves
- It is synthesis that transfers the learning activity to the student, rather than a teacher-directed activity

RX FOR THE COMMON CORE: RESEARCH CAPSULE FOR SYNTHESIS

A real-world moment:

Fifth graders researched the biographies of historical figures. Recording notes on names, places, dates, and geographic details, students had a plethora of factual information gathered and ready for their presentations. Standing in character, stock still, and costumed, they filled the multi-purpose room which had become a "Living Museum." Visitors poked the frozen presidents, pioneers, generals, suffragettes, and inventors. On cue, the poked figures began their litany of who, what, where, when details. The air was charged with frantic factoids. Afterward, the participants entertained questions about their historical characters. Questions about "most important contributions" were met with blank faces. When asked how the country would have been different without them, or what Lincoln might have said to Martin Luther King, only the blinking broke up the stillness. Although entertaining, this model's prognosis was ill due to lack of synthesis.

Synthesis is the glue. Isolated facts, details, or points transferred from notes to products have three downsides. One, as rote learning, they are quickly forgotten. Despite diligent coverage of a content topic, facts do not have shelf life or connections useful in new learning. Two, lacking connections to related and relevant big ideas, they do not build deep understanding. Three, without being manipulated, used, and applied in a knowledge product, they do not contribute to transfer or formative knowledge. Connecting facts, building big ideas, establishing relationships between big ideas, and eventually understanding complex concepts require synthesis.

Moving from surface facts to depth of understanding is the focus of the graphical representations that follow. In each case, educational research and experience regarding synthesis inform the ideas presented in charts, lists, and prompts. Concise, direct, visually enhanced, these graphical pages distill the ultimate teaching strategies for the Common Core.

See Appendix for the WISE Guide to Questioning, Synthesis, and Assessment.

7

Assessment

Information is not knowledge.

—Albert Einstein

EQ: How Do I Use Assessment for Learning?

A strong and emerging body of research based on *Balanced Assessment* points to the use of diagnostic, formative, and summative assessment tools to boost student performance. In addition, the notion of *next generation assessment* conveys the importance of authentic and performance-based assessment.

A grade on the top of a paper does not generally reflect the degree to which a child understands. The well-loved *Christmas Story* motion picture depicts young Ralphie languishing in Miss Shield's elementary classroom, having just been assigned a theme paper on "What I Want for Christmas." Much fantasizing ensues, and blazing success is anticipated with his brilliantly scripted pitch for a Red Rider air rifle. In a crushing turn of movie reality, Ralphie gets his work back with a C+ ensconced on the page and a warning about "shooting his eye out." What a blow to the ego, deflating ambition and motivation.

In a teacher-directed classroom, tasks are assigned, with more guidance than provided by Miss Shields. However, the Ralphies of the world often lack key elements for success, including models of quality products, ongoing formative assessment, and performance-based rubrics. The A++++++ that Ralphie dreamed of is not the product of chance, circumstance, hope, or misdirected effort. Success results from assessment for learning.

The phrase **assessment for learning** is widely used to convey the key role of assessment as a tool *for learning,* rather than just *evaluation.* Quality models that merge these strategies already exist in an array of resources such as those created by Intel, Jon Mueller, the City of New York, and a wiki based on Bloom called Educational Origami. Certainly apparent in the Common Core Learning Standards, these approaches to assessment are powerful, highly compatible, and solidly effective.

Establishing target skill levels and content knowledge through effective diagnostic assessment initiates a cycle of planned assessment. Research consistently points to the role of formative assessment for improved performance. A teacher who consults with students, elicits evidence of incremental skill development as projects are in progress, and clearly defines expectations, optimizing the success of learners. Students and their work are visible, present, and actively in progress. Gaps can be filled. Weak skill areas can be bolstered. Confusion can be clarified. And all of this can be implemented at the point of need.

The C+ scrawled on Raphie's theme is not an eloquent summary of his mediocre performance. No doubt Raphie's consternation and surprise match that of many learners who have few criteria for expected quality, no feedback in progress, and what might appear to be an arbitrary grade assigned. With intensity and single mindedness, educators have tested, tested, and tested again, as they complied with No Child Left Behind and other local data conventions. Former Commission of Education in New York, David Steiner, stated his support for the shift to new standards, because "assessment had become the curriculum."

EQ: How Do I Use
Assessment for Learning? (*Continued*)

When assessment is authentic and performance based, the active learner:

- Becomes an agent of personal success, connecting with his world
- Replaces passivity and powerlessness with stamina, responsibility, and measured progress
- Demonstrates understanding of content, synthesis of multiple information resources, and conclusions based on evidence
- Is measured in multiple ways such as rubrics, checklists, conferences, and relevant feedback contributing to a growing sense of what works for the learner
- Takes responsibility for achievement through learner-specific evaluation measures

Well-constructed summative assessments measure effectiveness of communication, mastery of content, attention to audience, purpose, and task, and use of technology. Eventually, a learner internalizes a model of successful strategies that continues to evolve. This set of skills and habits of mind become a part of the student who has *learned how to learn*. Motivation, engagement, creativity, and purpose are springboards for the application of essential knowledge and skills.

Research attests to the shallow, short term, and often plagiarized work produced by the disaffected learner, plowing through required work. A bureaucratic tasker performs at a level that rarely results in formative knowledge, mastery, or meaning. Research also documents that with the challenge of an authentic learning process (Inquiry), a dramatic shift in attitude and achievement occurs. When the Common Core Learning Standards weave rigor, depth, and relevance together as essential elements, the rationale for authentic work and assessment emerges eloquently.

The development of baseline measurements, ongoing formative assessments, midyear checks, and summative assessments will help teachers optimize the learning process. These assessments can indeed be performance based, student centered, authentic, and rigorous tools for learning. Inquiry learning experiences incorporate diagnostic, formative, and summative assessments guiding the learner to success throughout the process. The myth that Inquiry is not a form of guided instruction needs to be uprooted and replaced. Inquiry-based learning empowers the learner to achieve and measure his own progress, while being guided and instructed by his educators.

See the next section for an example of student self-assessment, as a formative assessment tool. ***Notice the language is in the first person, to empower the learner and shift responsibility.*** This rubric was included in a Common Core lesson where there was an evidence-based discussion after a short research assignment.

Persuasive Discussion—Communicating Effectively (Speaking and Language Standards)

We will be having an evidence-based discussion, or a Think Tank discussion. Using the following secondary rubric, evaluate yourself your participation. This rubric has 14 categories to demonstrate your positive communication characteristics when there are many contributors. Use this as a self-assessment or planning tool.

Smart choices: Consider your role during your discussion. Evaluate your participation based on the following thoughts: Were you . . . ? Or Did you . . . ?	✓Totally (7 points)	Somewhat (3.5 points)	Sorry, no. (0 points)	Notes
Prepared?				
Contribute?				
Cite evidence?				
Did my words support the position or oppose the position effectively? Or, were they wandering off the topic?				
Did my words include data or a quote?				
Did I consistently speak using correct grammar?				
Were my thoughts logical?				
Did I cite specific examples?				
Did I speak loudly and clearly?				
Did I look at my peers and make eye contact?				
Did I contribute new thoughts, and not mirror an old thought of someone else?				
Were my disagreements polite and diplomatic?				
Did I allow others to finish their thoughts before exchanging my point of view?				
Did I point out an agreement offering more evidence or a disagreement with different evidence?				

RX FOR THE COMMON CORE: RESEARCH CAPSULE FOR ASSESSMENT

A real-world moment:

The animal report with color pictures and a construction paper cover rests in a stack of school projects under the bed. The star sticker and "Nice job!" emblazoned on the front are good for a few feel good minutes. A ten page senior research paper with a C+ on the cover page, along with comments about bibliographic format and transition sentences, gets swept out with the knee deep debris of locker clean out. Nobody caught the cut and paste paragraphs. A quiz on a chapter in The Book Thief had a perfect score, thanks to a friendly text message and a picture of the test questions. Questioned about performance on a high stakes Power Point presentation, the group leader who had done the work said "I got 46 out of 50."

Assessment for learning requires diagnostic, formative, and summative assessment that is criteria referenced, authentic, and plugged into skills mastery and improved performance. Rubrics elucidate for teachers and learners the targets for learning. Evidence of mastery and deep understanding can be documented with well-crafted assessments. Multiple assessment measures bring to light what a learner knows and is able to do. Gaps and "not yet" areas benefit from a revised strategy for instruction. Self-assessment, peer review, and ongoing balanced assessment are all solidly built into the Common Core.

Moving from surface facts to depth of understanding is the focus of the graphical representations that follow. In each case, educational research and experience regarding assessment inform the ideas presented in charts, lists, and prompts. Concise, direct, visually enhanced, these graphical pages distill the ultimate teaching strategies for the Common Core.

Appendix for the WISE Guide to Questioning, Synthesis, and Assessment

Appendix

ACKNOWLEDGMENT

Hats off to David Ratzer for his creative graphic work on our curriculum books that breathed life into our Inquiry model.

WISE

EXPRESS
SYNTHESIZE
INVESTIGATE
WONDER

Guide to Questioning, Synthesis, and Assessment

Depth
Rigor
Relevance

Mining for Meaning

Inquiry Meets the Common Core

Today's millennial students are operating in a new mode of *transliteracy*—they read, uncover, and discover through a myriad of mediums. There is no longer a structure to reading and research. Students will read, watch, extract words, and synthesize from a variety of sources and source types. It is so imperative that we, as learning concierges, are able to guide students through the process of discovering meaning and drawing conclusions. This Inquiry process promotes higher-level thought, is aligned with the Common Core, replicates real-world problem solving strategies, and engages the student.

This *Guide to Questioning, Synthesis, and Assessment* has been written as a toolbox for this instructional paradigm shift. Use it wisely.

Questions, after all:
• are at the heart of Inquiry-based learning
• generate wonder and engagement
• drive deep authentic learning
• uncover meaning and connections
• and are the catalyst for synthesis and understanding

Questions help us *understand*, and questions help us assess. Good questioning techniques are vital to becoming a 21st-Century Instructor.

Can Your Seniors Do This?

Questioning and the Common Core

At the heart of all Inquiry is questioning. Deep questions, authentic questions, student-generated questions, critical analysis, and essential questions initiate and sustain Inquiry. Listed below is the "Inquiry" language within the common core.

- Conduct short as well as more sustained research projects based on focused questions, demonstrating understanding of the subject under investigation.

- Conduct short as well as more sustained research projects to answer a question (including a self-generated question) or solve a problem; narrow or broaden the Inquiry when appropriate; synthesize multiple sources on the subject, demonstrating understanding of the subject under investigation.

- Develop factual, interpretive, and evaluative questions for further exploration of the topic(s).

- Integrate and evaluate multiple sources of information presented in different media or formats (e.g., visually, quantitatively) as well as in words in order to address a question or solve a problem.

- Ask and answer questions about what a speaker says in order to clarify comprehension, gather additional information, or deepen understanding of a topic or issue.

- To be ready for college, workforce training, and life in a technological society, students need the ability to gather, comprehend, evaluate, synthesize, and report on information and ideas, to conduct original research in order to answer questions or solve problems, and to analyze and create a high volume and extensive range of print and nonprint texts in media forms old and new.

- Ask and answer such questions as *who, what, where, when, why,* and *how* to demonstrate understanding of key details in a text.

- Pose questions that connect the ideas of several speakers and respond to others' questions and comments with relevant evidence, observations, and ideas.

- Probe and reflect on ideas under discussion. Delineate a speaker's argument and specific claims, evaluating the soundness of the reasoning and relevance and sufficiency of the evidence and identifying when irrelevant evidence is introduced.

- Propel conversations by posing and responding to questions that probe reasoning and evidence; ensure a hearing for a full range of positions on a topic or issue; clarify, verify, or challenge ideas and conclusions; and promote divergent and creative perspectives.

http://www.corestandards.org

2

From *Rx for the Common Core: Toolkit for Implementing Inquiry Learning* by Mary Boyd Ratzer and Paige Jaeger. Santa Barbara, CA: Libraries Unlimited. Copyright © 2014.

Essential to Inquiry-Based Learning and Research

- prerequisites to learning
- a window into creativity and insight
- a catalyst for fresh thinking and a challenge to outdated assumptions.

Questions Are:

	Cognition	Products	Effect	Questions
Facts	Short-term recall Inert ideas Inflexible knowledge One right answer NO TRANSFER	Reports Worksheets Packets Scoop and spit	Disengaged Bureaucratic tasking Compliant No meaning No connections	Who What Where When
Explanation	Restating Information Related facts	Writing/ Speaking Using information With sense of relationships or organization Retelling	Task oriented Wants to be finished Goal is product, grade	Which What's different What's the same Can you define What is the main idea
Synthesis	Original conclusions Analysis of complex texts Integrate information Draw evidence Demonstrate understanding	Arguments to support claims Writing, speaking based on informational texts to support analysis, reflection, and research Narratives and Explanatory Texts	Engaged Active learner Negotiating questions Process products Meaning constructed Authentic intellectual work	Why How So what Should What if

Question types should move away from *Rote to dig deeper*

Questions Should Foster Higher-Level Thought

- **FACT Questions**—one right answer
- **Closed questions**—correct or incorrect, yes or no
- **Open questions**—defend, explain position
- **Follow-up questions**—clarification, limitless ideas, stir debate
- **Feedback questions**—focused, critical, redirect, stimulates reflection
- **Elaborate, hypothetical questions**—extend, WHAT IF, could, should
- **Essential questions**—probing, challenging, broad, enduring, encompassing the moral of the story, core of a content discipline, arguable, overarching, challenging, draw learners into the discipline
- **Powerful questions**—motivate fresh thinking, generate curiosity, stimulate thinking and conversation, surface and challenge assumptions, focus Inquiry, invite creativity, generate energy for exploration

Good Sample Questions

- What food groups did you eat today?
- What food groups are most important to health?
- Does this animal breathe air?
- Where does light come from?
- Why did Ahab chase Moby Dick?
- Should you modify your breakfast for more nutritional value?
- How does this animal breathe air?

- Why do we need light?
- How does the journey impact the destination?
- How did the sacrifices and convictions of individuals in the Civil War preserve the union?
- Why was Columbus a villain or hero?
- Should medical technology progress without ethical and moral considerations?
- How is man the measure of all things in the Renaissance?

From *Rx for the Common Core: Toolkit for Implementing Inquiry Learning* by Mary Boyd Ratzer and Paige Jaeger. Santa Barbara, CA: Libraries Unlimited. Copyright © 2014.

Socratic Questions are questions the teacher should ask to foster thought and curiosity

The Socratic Questioning technique is an effective way to explore ideas in depth. By *questioning*, teachers promote independent thinking and student ownership. Higher-level thinking skills are present while students think, discuss, debate, evaluate, and analyze.

Implication and consequence questions
- If that happened, what effect would it have?
- Would that probably happen, or definitely happen?
- If that happened, what else would happen as a result?
- What are the implications of this issue?
- What generalizations can you make?

Assumption questions
- What is being assumed here?
- Are there other assumptions that can be made instead?
- How can we verify that assumption? Disprove it?
- How did you make that assumption?

Origin or source questions
- What is the original source of this idea?
- Have you always held this view or has something influenced your thinking?
- How have related questions contributed to the development of this question?

Questions about the question or issue
- How important is this question? Why?
- Why do you think that this question is easy or difficult to answer?
- What does this question assume?
- How does this question generate other questions?

Viewpoint questions
- Why is this idea needed?
- How would different people respond to this question? Why?
- How would you respond to an objection from someone who disagrees?
- If someone believed _____ how would they react?
- What are alternatives to this view?

Clarification questions
- Why do you say that?
- What do you mean by that statement?
- Could you word that in another way?
- What is your main point?
- Could you give us an example, or explain further?

Reason and evidence questions
- Can you provide an example?
- How do you know this is true?
- What information or evidence supports this?
- Should you doubt your evidence?
- How did you reach this conclusion? What was your reasoning?
- What led you to that belief?
- What would change your mind?

From *Rx for the Common Core: Toolkit for Implementing Inquiry Learning* by Mary Boyd Ratzer and Paige Jaeger. Santa Barbara, CA: Libraries Unlimited. Copyright © 2014.

Student-Generated Questions

Golden Research Questions Need to be:

"NARROW and SPECIFIC, DEEP enough for multiple sources, COMPLEX enough for multiple points of view, BALANCED between fact and interpretation, STRUCTURED around different levels of questions including HOW, WHY, WHAT IF, SHOULD, and VARIED enough to address the richness of points of view, solutions, causes." – *New York City Information Skills Benchmarks*

"Without questions the Inquiry cycle stops and learning regresses into read and recite, without testing for relevance and meaning." – *Daniel Callison*

Students Need To Generate Questions For Digging Deep—Investigating

RED Light Questions	GREEN Light Questions
Question leads to one answer	Question leads to more information
Question leads to yes or no	You ask WHY, HOW, WHICH, WHAT IF
Question keeps you from thinking about more ideas	Question makes you investigate further, think, decide, validate thinking about more ideas
You already know the answer, or answer is rote	Question inspires ideas, new questions, new directions for research
Question is too broad or narrow	Question draws a personal response
Question is not interesting	Question leads to connections
Question requires lists or collections of facts	Question requires analysis, application of information, conclusions
Question STOPS with answer	Question makes you curious, engaged

Now with their own questions for research, students can go investigate.

Thinking and the Common Core

· Respond thoughtfully to diverse perspectives; synthesize comments, claims, and evidence made on all sides of an issue; resolve contradictions when possible; and determine what additional information or research is required to deepen the investigation or complete the task.

· Develop personal, cultural, textual, and thematic connections within and across genres as they respond to texts through written, digital, and oral presentations, employing a variety of media and genres.

· Analyze how a text makes connections among and distinctions between individuals, ideas, or events (e.g., through comparisons, analogies, or categories).

· Analyze a case in which two or more texts provide conflicting information on the same topic and identify where the texts disagree on matters of fact or interpretation. Use experience and knowledge of language and logic, as well as culture, to think analytically, address problems creatively, and advocate persuasively.

http://www.corestandards.org

As Students Investigate They Should Be Thinking

Thinking on a Continuum

OBVIOUS, scratches the surface, just uses what is given	Probes beyond the given, stretches for new connections, questions, applications
Fuzzy, rambling, unfocused, loses main ideas or purpose	Clear and focused, structured, clear purpose, tied to main ideas, organized
Simplistic, no detail or nuance, broad, general, simplified	Elaborated, richly detailed, imaginative, descriptive
One-dimensional, sees no complexity, layers, or viewpoints	Multidimensional, recognizes complexity, levels, perspectives, or viewpoints
Restricted, avoids big ideas or hard questions, biased, resistant	Generative, expands, extends, broadens, opens up new lines of Inquiry, curious
Tangential, strays from important, central ideas for trivia	Essence capturing, insightful, sees deep structure

Tishman, Shari. "Assessing Thinking: Six Continua" (Chart developed for the Artful Thinking Project, Project Zero, Harvard Graduate School of Education). Project Zero Website, May 9, 2013. http://www.old-pz.gse.harvard.edu/tc/content/assessment/6Continua.pdf.

From *Rx for the Common Core: Toolkit for Implementing Inquiry Learning* by Mary Boyd Ratzer and Paige Jaeger. Santa Barbara, CA: Libraries Unlimited. Copyright © 2014.

Synthesis
An Information → Knowledge Journey

America Is Raising the Bar on Thinking

Common Core

"Synthesize multiple sources on the subject, demonstrating understanding of the subject under investigation."

"Integrate information from several texts on the same topic in order to write or speak about the subject knowledgeably"

"Cite specific textual evidence to support analysis of primary and secondary sources, connecting insights gained from specific details to an understanding of the text as a whole."

INQUIRY Meets the Common Core

· Use facts to build meaning
· Connect ideas and information
· Think analytically, advocate persuasively
· Draw original conclusions
· Use vocabulary of the content knowingly
· Create products that convey new understanding

ISTE/AASL

Critical Thinking, Problem Solving, and Decision Making
Students use critical thinking skills to plan and conduct research, manage projects, solve problems, and make informed decisions. Students

· identify and define authentic problems and significant questions for investigation.
· plan and manage activities to develop a solution or complete a project.
· collect and analyze data to identify solutions and/or make informed decisions.
· use multiple processes and diverse perspectives to explore alternative solutions.

Research and Information Fluency
Students apply digital tools to gather, evaluate, and use information. Students

· plan strategies to guide Inquiry.
· locate, organize, analyze, evaluate, synthesize, and ethically use information from a variety of sources and media.
· evaluate and select information sources and digital tools based on the appropriateness to specific tasks.
· process data and report results.

Synthesis defined for the TEACHER

Understanding is being able to "teach it, use it, prove it, connect it, explain it, defend it, [and] read between the lines." - Wiggins and McTighe

T
- Students explore and culminate comprehension, application, and analysis
- Students create a knowledge product that exceeds and transforms the materials used

E
- Students fuse separate elements to form a coherent whole
- Students combine opposing and reinforcing ideas to make a new higher level of meaning

A
- Students combine elements or parts to recognize a pattern
- Students extract inferences that link what is found in logical, meaningful pattern
- Students use text to construct meaning, think deeply about ideas, and reason with evidence

C
- Students exhibit creativity
- Students' product is not just summary, paraphrase, or abstract
- Students generate unique communication

H
- Students' product is an analysis of information, facts, opinions, emotions, perceptions
- Students answer the questions: "What is most important? What is my conclusion?"

E
- Thesis is a strong statement that can be proven with evidence
- Thesis is a product of critical thinking after some research
- Perspective, point of view, voice needed to present conclusions

R
- Learners make sense of information by clarifying main and supporting ideas
- Learners look for patterns and connect ideas across resources
- Learners organize information by using a variety of tools and strategies
- Learners compare new ideas to prior knowledge and reflect on new understandings
- Learners draw conclusions by integrating new ideas with prior knowledge
- Learners discuss, collaborate, and negotiate meaning with others

Daniel Callison, Leslie Preddy
- *The Blue Book on Information Age Inquiry, Instruction and Literacy*

Barbara Stripling et al-
- *New York City Information Fluency Continuum*

T E A C H E R

Products generated
- arguments
- compositions
- conclusions
- confirmations
- decisions
- discoveries
- estimates
- explanations
- hypotheses
- insights
- inventions
- judgments
- performances
- plans
- predictions
- priorities
- probabilities
- problems
- products
- solutions
- representations
- resolutions
- results
- solutions

Required
- complex analysis
- creative thinking
- critical thinking
- decision making
- evaluation
- logical thinking
- metacognitive thinking
- problem solving
- reflective thinking
- scientific experimentation
- scientific Inquiry
- synthesis
- systems analysis

Knowledge products are the Common Core:
- Production and sharing of knowledge products
- Types of Text: Narratives, Expository, Arguments
- Integration of knowledge and ideas
- Respond to varying demands of audience, task, purpose, and discipline
- Collaboration and Communication

Start with
- ambiguities
- challenges
- confusions
- dilemmas
- discrepancies
- doubt
- obstacles
- paradoxes
- problems
- puzzles
- questions
- uncertainties

"Higher Order Skills – De?nition, Teaching Strategies, Assessment." http://www.cala.fsu.edu/files/higher_order_thinking_skills.pdf. Used with permission of Faranak Rohani, Director, Center for the Advancement of Learning and Assessment, Florida State University, Tallahassee, Florida

From *Rx for the Common Core: Toolkit for Implementing Inquiry Learning* by Mary Boyd Ratzer and Paige Jaeger. Santa Barbara, CA: Libraries Unlimited. Copyright © 2014.

Synthesis Strategies in Action

As Students Synthesize, They Construct New Knowledge

- Drawing conclusions or generalizing from facts, making inferences
- Supporting conclusions with evidence
- Drawing conclusions from looking at multiple perspectives
- Examples, quotes, data, textual references to support claims
- Explanation or analysis of evidence
- Extending thinking to create new ideas from old ones

Use these verbs to prompt SYNTHESIS!

T E A C H E R

Create	Invent	Compose	Predict	Organize
Plan	Construct	Design	Modify	Imagine
Elaborate	Combine	Original	Change	Adopt
Suppose	Improve	Produce	Set up	What if

"Synthesis." http://www1.center.k12.mo.us/edtech/Blooms/Synthesis.htm. Used with permission of Colleen McLain, Education Technology Specialist, Center School District, Kansas City, Missouri.

Getting to gold: Student guide to synthesis

S T U D E N T

DIG
- Find, read, and think about multiple, related informational texts
- Uncover the BIG PICTURE, gaps, conflicts, pros, cons

THINK
- Make sense of new, special, complex vocabulary
- Evaluate the quality of information and select the best
- Sort out different perspectives
- Determine fact and opinion
- Think critically to see relationships, logic, strongest arguments
- Begin to cluster related ideas, arguments, solutions
- Find and use details and pieces of evidence
- Sort out the best evidence and details
- Analyze information, facts, emotions, and perceptions
- Pull out BIG IDEAS, central argument, important issue

CONNECT
- Find relationships and connections among ideas, details
- Find logical, meaningful pattern in texts
- Cluster evidence and important arguments into categories
- Cluster ideas with similarities and differences and categorize
- Combine ideas in a new, original way
- Tie key solutions, arguments, and main ideas to a thesis
- Analyze related assumptions, points of view
- Combine ideas to make a new, original whole

CONCLUDE
- Decide on the central, essential issue, argument, idea
- State what is most important
- Present conclusions with a point of view
- Use complex vocabulary with understanding
- Decide on most relevant, useful evidence, detail
- Organize/sequence relevant BIG IDEAS with related detail
- Considering facts, data, evidence, draw a conclusion
- Cogently state conclusions with depth and meaning
- Go beyond paraphrasing, summarizing, and restating
- Unify elements in a new pattern proposing alternatives

The Information to Knowledge Journey: how do you know when you strike gold?

STUDENT

- Move beyond gathered facts, stockpiles, disconnected surface grasp of details
- Students move beyond a superficial sense of relationships between facts
- Reach meaningful, original conclusions
- Organize coherently, reflecting a sense of how ideas relate to each other
- Use their mind to transform text, not simply transfer text
- Use content vocabulary in knowledge products and writing demonstrating understanding
- Address discrepancies, reconcile conflicts, explore oppositional ideas
- Synthesize multiple perspectives and texts to build evidence
- Treat a subject area creatively
- Establish personal conclusions using found information
- Have a strong awareness of information quality
- Condense sets of facts into fewer but more abstract statements
- Exhibit interest, motivation, empathy, self-knowledge
- Engage in critical analysis and communication
- Develop arguments, viewpoints, positions
- Use evidence, data, arguments that are appropriate
- Provide evidence of deep questions
- Use technology tools effectively to communicate new knowledge
- Students own the process
- Move from description to detailed explanation
- Increase specificity of topic focus
- Can give personal estimate of how much is known
- Integrate and unify ideas
- Develop ideas with structural centrality and unity

Used with permission of Ross Todd, PhD,
Director, Center for International Scholarship in School Libraries,
School of Communications and Information, Rutgers University, New Brunswick, NJ

Strategies for Synthesis:
Digging Deep into Information and Mining for Meaning

STUDENT

Analyze information for:

- Cause and effect
- Conclusions
- Categories
- Relationships
- Patterns
- Hierarchies
- Relevance
- Irrelevance
- Value
- Comparisons
- Contrasts
- Key concept
- Bias

Ask questions as you read:

How is this organized?

Can I map or outline this?

Do I agree or disagree?

What supports this point?

What evidence is needed to prove this?

Who would disagree with this?

What information is needed to proceed?

What is the point of view?

How does this relate to other facts, data, or evidence I have?

How important is this?

As Students Investigate, They Should Synthesize

From *Rx for the Common Core: Toolkit for Implementing Inquiry Learning* by Mary Boyd Ratzer and Paige Jaeger. Santa Barbara, CA: Libraries Unlimited. Copyright © 2014.

Assessment to Transform Learning and Teaching

Traditional
Multiple choice
Recall, recognize
Indirect evidence
Teacher-directed

UNCOVER
DISCOVER
TRANSFORM

Authentic
Performance
Connections
Real world
Construct meaning
Direct evidence

Authentic Assessment Defined

"A form of assessment in which students are asked to perform real-world tasks that demonstrate meaningful application of essential knowledge and skills." –**Jon Mueller**

"…Engaging and worthy problems or questions of importance, in which students must use knowledge to fashion performances effectively and creatively. The tasks are either replicas of or analogous to the kinds of problems faced by adult citizens and consumers or professionals in the field." –**Grant Wiggins** (Wiggins, 1993, p. 229)

"Based on performance and reality, authentic assessment allows for learner specific evaluation, self-assessment, measures meaningful and valid tasks, is criterion referenced, and is implemented with **a wide variety of tools.**" –**University of Alberta**

How do I design AUTHENTIC ASSESSMENT? Do I have the tools?

Assessment and Achievement

I Need to Asses at the Beginning, Middle, and End

Diagnostic	Formative	Summative
To inform instruction	To inform learning	To measure knowledge
Measures pre-existing knowledge and skills	Guides teacher decision making and improves instruction	Gauges progress, mastery of content and skills
Occurs early in the teaching cycle, and during it	Tools to generate ongoing evidence of understanding	Evaluates effectiveness of instruction, innovates
Determines specific learning needs in relation to expectations	Can help learner self-assess	Learners demonstrate knowledge in many ways

Teaching to the Test focuses on the recall of surface information vs. deep, flexible content mastery.

"The act of teaching to the test limits the teacher's ability to use multiple creative teaching methods based on their students' needs (Riffert, 2005) and creates an atmosphere of learning facts and material without any real emphasis on student understanding beyond the ability to answer test questions correctly" (Posner, 2004).

Diagnostic

Survey the learning landscape—Assess before teaching to plan instruction and the learning process.

- Captures prior knowledge and skills with evidence
- Brainstorming, discussing, mind mapping, concept mapping
- KWL Chart
- Think-Pair-Share, Peer questioning
- Charting or lists for categorizing
- Shared observations, student questions, ideas
- Word walls with subject focus
- Anticipation guide, graphic organizers
- Misconception, assumption analysis

Uncover—How are students progressing? How should I adjust my teaching? Are target skills evident?

- Student answers the questions—"Am I getting it? How am I doing?" Self-management!
- Student plans research, makes strategic decisions based on criteria and feedback
- Infused throughout the learning continuum
- Foster reviews from peers, teacher conferencing

Discover—Student demonstrates understanding and skill to capture and report achievement.

- Student constructs a tangible, substantial product by analyzing, evaluating, and synthesizing
- New knowledge emerges as student engages with quality texts in multiple formats
- Evidence from texts supports strong arguments, original conclusions
- Student demonstrates meaningful answers to important questions

Formative

TEACHER-Led Formative Assessment	LEARNER-Led Formative Assessment
Ungraded exams, journal prompts	**Reflecting**—Learning log, Tag Toss, Progress log, I CAN Statements, Journal, Blog, What worked? 3-2-1
Feedback on drafts, observation	**Questioning**—Generating questions, Inquiry framework questions, Question stems, Question Webs
Exit cards, approval stages	**Organizing**—Visualization, concept map, simplified outline, goal setting, project plans, donuts, notes TARGET
Observation checklist/rubrics	**Sharing**—Reciprocal teaching, think aloud, THINK PAIR SHARE, learning communities, group assessment
Consultation, informal interview, conference agenda	**Challenging**—Peer review and feedback, What if, Why, What else, Who says questions, HERE'S What, So What, Now What?
Benchmarks check	**Evaluating**—Rubric, checklist, Rating Scale
Interactive research journal, wiki	**Internalizing**—Assimilating process skills, thinking skills, transparent thinking, summaries, topic sentences

Used with permission of Barbara Stripling, Professor of Practice, School of Information Studies, Syracuse University, former Director of the New York City School Library System

From *Rx for the Common Core: Toolkit for Implementing Inquiry Learning* by Mary Boyd Ratzer and Paige Jaeger. Santa Barbara, CA: Libraries Unlimited. Copyright © 2014.

Summative

Assessing Knowledge Products and Performance in the 21st Century

Conduct an original experiment

- Video, Multimedia and Photo Journals
- Student-led conferences
- Models, exhibits, prototypes, blueprints
- Letters, diaries, community publication
- Reenactment
- Public Service Announcement
- Newscasts

Perform an original skit, dance, role play

- Narratives, scripts, poetry, digital story telling
- Cartoons, comics, murals, infographic
- Debate, mock trial, speeches
- Musical composition
- Media sharing
- E-portfolio
- Podcast

Presentation, iMovie, Voice Thread, Debate, Talk Show, Speech, Interview

- Argument, persuasive proposal with evidence
- Teaching or mentoring
- Vlog, Blog, Website, Prezi
- Forum, Desk Top Sharing
- Voice Thread, Crazy Talk
- Photostory, Animoto

ISTE-Educational technology standards are the roadmap to teaching effectively and growing professionally in an increasingly digital world. Technology literacy is a crucial component of modern society. In fact, the globalizing economy and technological advances continue to place a premium on a highly skilled labor force.

EXPRESS
SYNTHESIZE
INVESTIGATE
WONDER

Assessing Teaching Practice, Inquiry Planning, Unit Plans

As I Teach, I Should Self-Assess

Have I...

- Determined and communicated learning goals for higher-order thinking skills?
- Addressed learning standards? Rigor?
- Tapped prior knowledge and built background?
- Emphasized connections, explicit or inferred?
- Promoted student thinking?
  - Interpreting facts
  - Synthesizing information
  - Reasoning logically
  - Framing arguments with evidence
- Promoted student questioning? Deep levels of questioning?
- Used organization tools, mapping, charts, timelines?
- Developed criteria for evaluating information, relative importance and relevance of ideas?
- Engendered debate and discussion?
- Focused on essential question and focus questions?
- Provided paths to investigation? Choices?
- Mentored and guided self-directed students?
- Promoted active, authentic quest for new ideas authentic questions, resources, products?
- Integrated original conclusions?
  - Test against evidence
  - Divergent/convergent thinking
  - Relative strength of arguments, positions, perspectives
  - Critical stance
- Planned and implemented multiple, ongoing assessments?
- Incorporated technology?
- Framed a final knowledge product that is publicly presented?
- Utilized models and criteria in advance?

EQ: What Is the WISE Curriculum?

WISE is an acronym for **Wonder, Investigate, Synthesize, Express**.

The WISE Inquiry Model Teacher's Guide that follows is a roadmap to Inquiry-based instruction and planning. Widely used as a basis for professional development, **WISE** walks collaborating teachers, school librarians, and special educators into the process of implementing Inquiry. The **WISE** steps clearly delineated performance indicators, teaching tools, assessment tools, BIG IDEAS, and a baseline of research for each of the four steps in Inquiry for younger learners.

Providing a script for the planning of an Inquiry-based learning experience, **WISE** is compact, diligently grounded in successful curricular models, and speaks eloquently to those motivated to initiate a shift to Inquiry in their classroom or library. Selections of tools for essential question development, knowledge product design, self-assessment, and higher-level thinking are part of **WISE**. Extensive use of this guide in the field with many hundreds of educators has proven its value as productive, effective, and as a user-friendly passport to best practice.

A more complex model is included in this book as well, **Inquiry Based Curriculum: Library and Information Skills for 21st-Century Learners.** The complex model states student dispositions, or what teachers should observe, when a learner is actively engaged in the learning process.

WISE

WONDER · INVESTIGATE · SYNTHESIZE · EXPRESS

Inquiry Model Teacher's Guide

This curriculum was developed to serve as a guide for teachers stepping into Inquiry or collaborative research models for the 21st-century learner. This is a simple model to enrich the student's learning experience and support academic success. Inquiry is not a "clean" fill-in-the-blank research model where students search for facts a teacher–leader has predefined, but Inquiry places the student in charge of his learning direction. Inquiry fosters student ownership of the process and student pride in the product. This works.

In a well-defined Inquiry unit, the teacher serves as a learning concierge and academic guide ensuring that learning goals are met and content vocabulary is understood. Inquiry is an authentic way of learning that is driven by questioning, thoughtful investigation, synthesizing information, and developing new understandings. This is characterized by student-centered exploration, engagement, social interaction, communication, and performance-based assessment.

WISE Inquiry

WONDER

·

INVESTIGATE
information

·

SYNTHESIZE

·

EXPRESS

WISE

WONDER · INVESTIGATE · SYNTHESIZE · EXPRESS

Wisdom
for Teachers

WE BELIEVE...

- **START** with compelling content
- Develop **BACKGROUND KNOWLEDGE**
- Connect to the learner's **REAL WORLD**
- Build on quality **QUESTIONS**
  - Essential questions
  - Guiding questions
  - Student questions
- Authentic learners need **CHOICES**
- Authentic learners have **VOICES**
- **THINKING** is fundamental
- **ENGAGED** learners care and count
- **CHALLENGE** leads to depth of understanding
- **SOCIAL INTERACTION** boosts success
- **COMMUNICATION** and sharing build learning communities
- **NEW KNOWLEDGE** is the goal
- Wise learners **REFLECT** and **EVALUATE**
- Wise teachers **ASSESS** and provide ongoing feedback

> "Inquiry gives me wings."
>
> -Taylor, 4th grade, Karigon Elementary

From *Rx for the Common Core: Toolkit for Implementing Inquiry Learning* by Mary Boyd Ratzer and Paige Jaeger. Santa Barbara, CA: Libraries Unlimited. Copyright © 2014.

WONDER

Indicators for a 21st-Century elementary learner:

- Shares what he/she knows about topic, problem, or concept
- Explores and connects ideas to his/her world
- Acquires background information
- Identifies key terms related to the topic
- Identifies key concepts related to the topic
- Asks clarifying questions
- Makes connections to the "big picture"
- Develops awareness of expectations/criteria components of final product
- Identifies purpose for using information
- Asks/creates questions about the topic with guidance
- Uses key concepts/terms to guide Inquiry
- Brainstorms keywords and synonyms for the intended topic
- Brainstorms possible sources of Information
- Identifies intended audience

Teacher Tools

- Read-in
- Video or videoclip
- Jackdaw (primary source materials)
- Photographs
- Internet tour, field trip
- Word Wall
- Speaker/demonstration
- ABC Power Point
- Teacher's Trunk
- Immersion in multiple sources of information
- Envisioning guide
- Electronic picture book
- KWL with emphasis on K
- Videoconference Brainstorming (chart paper, Inspiration)
- Generate questions, question web
- Concept mapping
- Webbing
- Anticipation guide

Wonder Assessment Tools

- KWL Charts
- Graphic organizers
- Think/Pair/Share
- One minute writing tasks
- Learning logs
- Observation log
- I Notice, I Know, I Wonder
- Facilitated conversation

Wonder BIG Ideas!

Activate thinking

Generate curiosity

Build background information

Tap prior knowledge

Frame quality questions for investigation

Research Says

- Children come to school naturally curious but lose curiosity in content coverage models.
- Encouraging students to form their own questions has a positive impact on learning.
- Students are likely to face the task of creating questions with uncertainty.
- Questions requiring low-level thinking encourage copying and regurgitating answers.
- Engaging students with quality questions is a strong indicator of success for the learner.
- Connecting new learning with background knowledge, prior knowledge and experience, and vocabulary will result in improved performance.
- CHOICES and student-directed process engage and motivate learners.
- Metacognition, or modeling thought, will help teach students how to think.

INVESTIGATE INFORMATION

Indicators for a 21st-Century elementary learner:

Find
- Understands and uses information environments (i.e., libraries, computers, people, etc.)
- Creates a list of search/keywords related to topic
- Locates resources in different formats for individual level of understanding
- Uses library catalogs and appropriate search engines, online databases, Internet search tools for finding information
- Connects personal knowledge and information from a variety of sources, genres, points of view, and formats to construct the "big picture"

Think
- Uses print or digital sources with increasing confidence
- Uses reading and thinking strategies to build meaning
- Distinguishes between fact and opinion
- Selects and records appropriate information in an effective note-taking process
- Takes notes using student's own words
- Recognizes conflicting facts, opposing ideas, and gaps in information
- Identifies main idea and supporting details
- Works collaboratively in a group
- Writes, draws, or verbalizes the main idea

Review
- Evaluates sources to be CAR: Credible, Accurate, Reliable
- Reviews and refocuses as necessary
- Uses information and technology ethically and responsibly
- Checks progress to generate conclusions, connections, and new ideas

Investigate BIG Ideas!

Construct meaning from text
·
Use facts to build big ideas
·
Manage search process
·
Record information using own words
·
Determine relationship between ideas

Teacher Tools

- Talk to your librarian
- Use pathfinders
- Create a search strategy
- Skim and scan
- Read for information
- Brainstorm where and how to find information
- Gather information
- Take notes using graphic organizers

WISE

Investigate Assessment Tools

- Checklists
- Process rubrics
- Semantic maps
- Plan development organizer
- Brainstorming Webs
- Graphic organizers
- T-charts
- Inference sharing
- Evaluating resources, ideas
- Marginal notes
- Draw pictures
- Response journals
- Two column note taking:
    - Notes/Reflections
    - Main ideas/Details, Examples
    - Ideas from text/Connections to prior knowledge
- Writing questions about text
- Writing new questions after reading
- Learning logs
- Exit cards
- Observation checklists
- Conferencing
- Peer evaluation

Research Says

- Children are resourceful in easy searches, but lack the skills to formulate search strategies.
- Children need content knowledge before they can develop search terminology.
- Children need direct instruction to develop search skills and evaluative thinking.
- The level of search complexity can be changed as children mature.

SYNTHESIZE

Indicators for a 21st-Century elementary learner:

- Organizes and communicates main and supporting ideas
- Offers examples, data, and details to support ideas
- Connects and compares ideas from various sources
- Connects information with prior knowledge
- Describes/explains relationships among ideas
- Resolves any conflicting information, opposing ideas, and/or gaps in information
- Gathers additional information as needed
- Demonstrates understanding of new knowledge, supported by evidence

Teacher Tools

- Planning presentation
- Review assessment criteria, rubric
- Cooperative learning
- Model quality products
- Organize notes
- Create an outline
- Draft, assess, revise
- Conferencing and questioning (teacher-to-student, student-to-teacher, and student-to-student)
- Compare new ideas to prior ideas, compare evidence to hypothesis

Synthesize Assessment Tools

- Chart concepts, relationships among ideas
- Use of evidence from text to support inferences
- Use of vocabulary from the content
- Quick writes or directed writing
- New questions
- Process checklists/rubrics
- Product checklists/rubrics

Synthesize BIG Ideas!

Using facts to build meaning

•

Connecting ideas

•

Determining relationships between ideas

•

Drawing conclusions

•

Differentiating important or central ideas

•

Using the vocabulary of the content knowingly

•

Designing and creating a product that conveys new understanding

Research Says

- Children are naturally predisposed to thinking and creating abilities.
- Teaching of summarization skills contributes to success in drawing original conclusions.
- Creativity can be reawakened in children through teaching strategies and Inquiry process.
- Children need to own their own content.
- Thinking can be enhanced by concept maps of various kinds as learners encounter important ideas. Comparing, contrasting, judging, and testing ideas across information sources lead to understanding relationships between ideas.
- Learners contruct meaning from text using information literacy skills.

EXPRESS

Indicators for a 21st-Century elementary learner:

- Shows understanding of material
- Understands differences/benefits of presentation formats
- Uses elements of standard citations
- Includes writing process to develop expression of new understanding
- Begins/develops understanding of critique process
- Uses feedback to improve presentation
- Rehearses and practices presentation

Teacher Tools

- Rehearses
- Embeds choice of presentation formats
- Uses feedback to edit
- Videotapes, critiques
- Shares, presents, engages critical questions

Express Assessment Tools

- Presentation rubric with specific criteria
- Writing process tools for revision, edit
- Literate conversations
- Student collaborations to assess arguments or conclusions
- Question development for further research

Research Says

- Communicating has intrinsic benefits for learners.
- These benefits include increased confidence, the discovery of "voice," new experience, and improved competence.
- Sharing original products in a climate of critical engagement boosts motivation and concern regarding quality of work.
- Students who learn to communicate in a variety of media and technological platforms learn the tool skills of production in that media.

EXPRESS BIG Ideas!

Communicate new knowledge

Use appropriate format for audience

Critical engagement of audience

Self-assess and revise product based on feedback

Communicate clearly main and supporting points

Encourage student freedom of expression through many modalities and technologies

Encourage creativity

Roadmap for Planning for a Collaborative Research Unit
Information-Infused Investigation

Librarian and classroom teacher do the work

1. **Begin with the end in mind:** (backward design, Wiggins & McTighe)
   Collaborate with teachers in planning, if possible.
   - What do you want your students to know (or be able to do) when they are finished?
   - What is the core content?
   - What is (are) the Common Core learning standard(s) I want to hit?
   - What information literacy skills will you focus on during this unit?
     - AASL 21st Century Standards
     - ISTE Standards (if your school has embraced these)

2. **Identify Essential Content Vocabulary**
   Teacher provides the vocabulary needed for assessment, useful for research, and expected to be seen (or heard) in the students' knowledge product(s).

3. **Teacher "sets the stage"**
   - How will I introduce this project?
   - What background knowledge do students need?
   - Do I need to preteach essential background? Skills?

4. **Develop the Investigation "big question" for the project to inspire student learning/interest.**

5. **Plan & deliver pre-assessment strategies:**
   - Classroom teacher's content
   - Librarian preassessment of IL skills
   - Librarian identifies:
     - IL skills needed
     - EQs for instruction
     - Resource potential

Students do the work

6. **Students Generate research questions.**
   - Activate thinking
   - Imbed meaning
   - Connect to student's world

7. **Research ... investigation**
   - What resources will students use?
   - Websites, books, databases, etc.

8. **What is the final (knowledge) project?**

Teachers and students

9. **How will I assess student learning?**

10. **Reflect on the process when the unit is complete**
    - What will I do differently next time?

From *Rx for the Common Core: Toolkit for Implementing Inquiry Learning* by Mary Boyd Ratzer and Paige Jaeger. Santa Barbara, CA: Libraries Unlimited. Copyright © 2014.

Goal: Higher-Level THINKING, PRODUCTS, QUESTIONS

LEVEL	VERBS	PRODUCTS	QUESTIONS
Synthesizing	Build, create, design, develop, devise, generate, hypothesize, invent, propose, theorize, compose, construct, invent, improve, adapt, imagine, formulate	A model program to address social issue; inventing a new animal; creating a new country; designing a building, machine, process, experiment; developing legislation; devising an ethical code, a way to test a new concept or theory; creating a play, a song, a movie	What if? Why? How? Should? So what?
Transforming	Blend, build, combine, compile, conclude, compose, convince, decide, dramatize, express, forecast, imagine, modify, revise	Ad campaign, a board game, a poem or short story, a play, dialog, speech, role play, news show, historical newspaper, Web page	What is your: Conclusion? Connection? Prediction?
Challenging	Appraise, argue, assess, criticize, compare, debate, defend, judge, justify, rank, prioritize, refute, review, support, value, weigh, verify, recommend	Critical review, argue as an attorney, determine the worth of a project, defend a judgment, debate issues, evaluate information, investigate a problem, justify a rank	Which is better? How would you rate? Refute? What evidence Supports?
Analyzing	Analyze, apply, associate, break down, differentiate, change, compare, contrast, distinguish, examine, infer, experiment, relate, select, map, sift, solve	Create a timeline or flowchart and correlate events, transplant an event or person, write an obituary or review, letter to the editor, rewrite w/ new perspective, graphic	Why do you think? What justifies? How is this related? How can you distinguish?
Explaining	Cite, complete, describe, document, explain, expand, give examples, illustrate, restate, paraphrase, generalize, show, solve, use, portray	Dramatize, illustrate, present a news show, fictional diary or narrative, resume for a person researched, explorer's log, journal, guided tour	What? Who? Where? When? What is different, the same?
Recalling	Arrange, cluster, find, identify, label, list, locate, match, name, recall, reproduce, select, state, recount	Select or list, find facts, select pictures, state questions of a reporter, arrange words, define words, write a letter recounting, chart facts, make a timeline	Who? What? Where? When?

Based on the REACTS Taxonomy by Barbara Stripling and Judy Pitts and Bloom's Taxonomy.

From *Rx for the Common Core: Toolkit for Implementing Inquiry Learning* by Mary Boyd Ratzer and Paige Jaeger. Santa Barbara, CA: Libraries Unlimited. Copyright © 2014.

What's the moral of the story?

Finding the perfect question that will drive student investigation and learning is difficult. The more you brainstorm, the better you become at framing a question that will compel deep learning, foster student ownership, and meet learning objectives.

Listed below are a few precepts.

Essential questions:

- Are arguable and important
- Are at the heart of the subject
- Often start with HOW? WHY? WHICH? WHAT IF? SHOULD? SO WHAT?
- Recur in school and in life
- Raise more questions
- Often raise important issues
- Can provide a purpose for learning
- Require meaning beyond understanding and studying, some kind of resolve or action, making a choice or forming a decision
- Cannot be answered by a few words, yes or no
- Probably shift and evolve
- May be unanswerable
- Will serve a unifying core for plan

ESSENTIAL QUESTION:

_____

_____

_____

SAMPLES:

- How were the 1930s and 1940s a period of forced change?
- How has racism affected the culture and history of the United States?
- How has the United States changed because of the Age of Exploration?
- What if we lost World War II?
- How should bioethics guide emerging scientific technology?
- How does conflict cause literary characters to grow?
- How can literature inspire us to face adversity?
- How did European contact challenge Native peoples of New York?
- Why has the Hudson River written the history of Eastern New York?
- What do living things need to survive?
- How has the earth changed over time?

From *Rx for the Common Core: Toolkit for Implementing Inquiry Learning* by Mary Boyd Ratzer and Paige Jaeger. Santa Barbara, CA: Libraries Unlimited. Copyright © 2014.

KNOWLEDGE product design

Students should have a platform to communicate:

- Ideas
- Arguments
- Their own synthesis and conclusions

Students should have an opportunity to demonstrate their expertise:

- By using core content vocabulary in knowledge product
- By discussing relationships in ideas, connections
- Answering questions central to the issue
- Citing rich information sources
- Demonstrating rigor vs. rote

Knowledge products:

- Showcases the students' analysis and synthesis
- Demonstrate personal understanding
- Encourages transfer and sharing of conclusions

KNOWLEDGE product:

Avoid Information Products that have these characteristics:

- Knowledge remains on a factual level
- Squirreling, stockpiling
- Easiest part of the search process is access
- Information seeking merely collecting facts
- Information overload
- Student is relieved when project is complete
- Low levels of interest and engagement
- Bureaucratically completing tasks (A. Zamuda, 2009)
- Missing "meaning"
- Partial or insufficient background knowledge
- No connection to life or prior learning
- Little evaluation
- Missing relevant documents

INQUIRY EVIDENCE:

How will we ACTIVATE and sustain thinking?

How will we build background and integrate prior knowledge?

How will we ENGAGE the learner? Activate thinking?

How will we make our plan STUDENT CENTERED?

How will we reach the goal of deep understanding and content mastery?

How are we using formative assessment to boost performance?

How will we achieve MEANINGFUL learning?

How will we share our products with meaningful audiences?

Prepared with students in mind.

Inquiry Model Teacher's Guide

Inquiry

Building minds to meet tomorrow's challenges

WISE Inquiry Model
© Copyright 2012

EQ: Where Did This Inquiry Curriculum Come From?

In 2006, school librarians gathered in the Capital Region of New York State to create an information literacy curriculum. As the instructional role of the school librarian ascended, the need for a common curricular platform also increased. The courage to move from the known to the unknown characterized this group of professionals.

Inquiry learning inspired change. The big shift to a student-negotiated, question-driven, wonder-generating research process took on skin and bones in this curriculum. Adopting the Inquiry approach to information literacy left more than one librarian with uncertainty and angst, but the road to Inquiry was paved by the document that follows.

In this curriculum, performance indicators, dispositions for the learner, and self-assessment questions guide the learner through the process. This curriculum set the standard of genuine synthesis, shared knowledge products, social and ethical responsibilities of the learner.

This curriculum and the WISE curriculum is widely used around New York State and was based upon the contributions of over 150 librarians from over New York and was influenced by the work of Barbara Stripling.

Inquiry-Based Curriculum:
Library and Information Skills for 21st-Century Learners

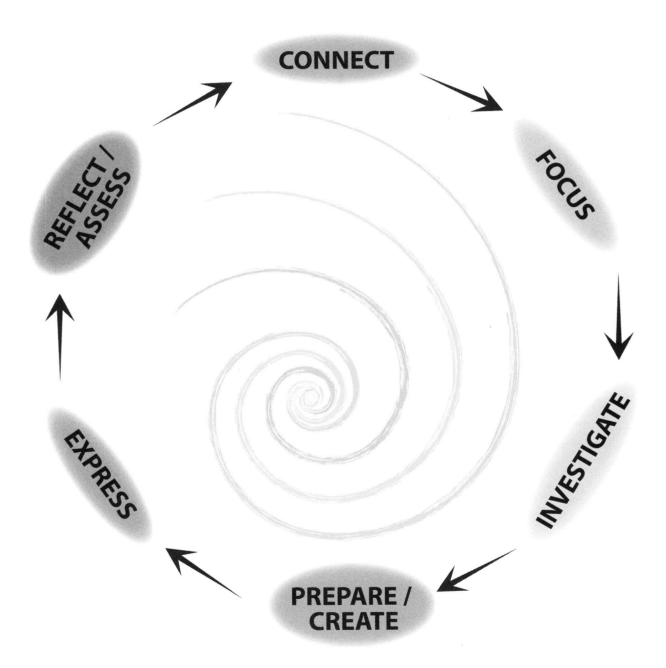

From *Rx for the Common Core: Toolkit for Implementing Inquiry Learning* by Mary Boyd Ratzer and Paige Jaeger. Santa Barbara, CA: Libraries Unlimited. Copyright © 2014.

Twenty-first century learners will use Inquiry to build understanding.

"I am a thinker."

Inquiry provides a framework for learning. An independent learner asks questions and accesses, evaluates, and uses information effectively to develop new understandings.

INQUIRY PHASE: EXPLORE and CONNECT

Key Dispositions of the 21st-Century Learner:

- Curiosity
- Engagement
- Active participation
- Adaptability
- Self-direction

At the beginning of the Connect Phase, a student may ask:

- What interests me about this idea or topic?
- What do I already know or think I know about this topic?
- What background information would help me get an overview of my topic?

INDICATORS—21st-Century Learner:

- Explores and connects ideas to self; finds personal meaning.
- Connects ideas to previous experience and knowledge.
- Acquires background information and knowledge of context through observation, experience, and reading.
- Identifies key concepts and terms related to the topic.
- Identifies the "big picture" and how it connects to the world.
- Asks clarifying questions.
- Recognizes the need for information.
- Develops an awareness of criteria and components of final product.

Before moving to the Focus Phase, a student may ask:

- Do I know enough about the idea or topic to ask good questions?
- Am I interested enough in the idea or topic to investigate it?
- Can I state what I know about the topic, problem, or big ideas?

INQUIRY PHASE: FOCUS

***Key Dispositions of the
21st-Century Learner:***

- Confidence
- Self-direction
- Adaptability
- Persistence
- Questioning
  - Seeking information about new ideas
  - Inquisitiveness

***At the beginning of the
Focus Phase, a student may ask:***

- Why am I doing this investigation?
  - What do I expect to find?
- What are the questions I need to answer?
- What kind of product will I be creating,
  and who is my audience?

INDICATORS—21st-Century Learner:

- Indentifies purpose for Inquiry.
- Maintains an awareness of final product (criteria and components).
- Determines intended audience.
- Formulates preliminary questions and ideas to focus on.
- Develops research questions, thesis, or hypothesis to guide Inquiry.
- Distinguishes the types of information needed to answer questions
  with relevant, appropriate sources.
  - Refines, focuses, and limits scope of the question.

Before moving to the Investigate Phase, a student may ask:

- Do my questions lead me to answers that
  will fulfill my assignment?
- What kind of information will be useful
  to my final product?

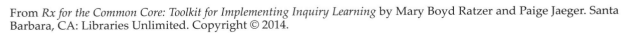

From *Rx for the Common Core: Toolkit for Implementing Inquiry Learning* by Mary Boyd Ratzer and Paige Jaeger. Santa Barbara, CA: Libraries Unlimited. Copyright © 2014.

INQUIRY PHASE: INVESTIGATE

Key Dispositions of the 21st-Century Learner:
- Personal productivity
- Self-direction—self-monitoring
- Adaptability
- Persistence
- Personal responsibility
- Truth seeking
- Team work / collaboration
- Strategic action
- Motivation

At the beginning of the Investigate Phase, a student may ask:
- What are all of the sources that might be used?
- Which sources will be most useful and valuable?
- How do I locate these sources?
- How do I find the information within each source?
- How do I evaluate the information that I find?

INDICATORS—21st-Century Learner:

ACCESS:
- Applies background knowledge to understand libraries and information environments.
- Locates desired resources within all information environments.
- Identifies and uses appropriate resources in print and digital formats.
- Uses indexes, catalogs, and other search tools to access relevant print or digital information.
- Uses organizational features in both print and digital resources.
- Locates information from diverse sources, genres, points of view, and formats to construct the big picture.

ANALYZE:
- Uses print or digital sources competently for Inquiry.
- Refines and expands synonyms and keywords related to the topic.
- Uses reading and thinking strategies to comprehend information and construct meaning.
- Uses visual literacy strategies to derive meaning from visual information and media.
- Interprets, evaluates, and appreciates visual information and media.
- Selects and records appropriate information in reflective and interactive process.
- Puts information into own words.
- Analyzes information from multiple, varied sources and formats for usefulness and relevance.
- Reconciles contradictions, opposing ideas, gaps in information.
- Participates productively in groups to define problems and pursue information.

ASSESS:
- Critically evaluates information sources for bias, relevance, accuracy, reliability, and authority
- Monitors progress and changes direction as necessary.
- Self-assesses for ethical use of intellectual and creative property.
- Checks progress to generate conclusions, connections, and new ideas.

Before moving to the Construct/Create Phase, a student may ask:
- Have I located sources with diverse perspectives?
- Have I found enough accurate information to answer all my questions?
- Have I discovered information gaps and filled them with more research?
- Have I begun to identify relationships and patterns and thoughtfully reacted to the information I found?

From *Rx for the Common Core: Toolkit for Implementing Inquiry Learning* by Mary Boyd Ratzer and Paige Jaeger. Santa Barbara, CA: Libraries Unlimited. Copyright © 2014.

INQUIRY PHASE: CONSTRUCT/CREATE

Key Dispositions of the
21st-Century Learner:
- Critical thinking
- Confidence
- Adaptability
- Engagement
- Persistence
- Seeking perspectives
- Collaboration
- Critical stance
- Creativity

At the beginning of the
Construct/Create Phase, a student may ask:
- What does the information mean? How can I organize the information? Is all of the information useful?
- What is the main idea? What is the evidence that supports the main idea?
- What are the similarities and differences among the sources? Is there contradictory information? How can I resolve the differences?
- How does the new information compare to my earlier knowledge?
- How do my ideas connect with each other?
- How have my ideas changed as a result of my investigation?
- Does the new information agree with my thesis?
- Do I need more information? Do I need to revise my thesis?
- What conclusions can I draw from my evidence? What examples show that my evidence supports my conclusions?
- Which parts of my problem solving process were successful? Which resources gave me valuable information?
- Am I ready to create a first draft?

INDICATORS—21st-Century Learner:
- Understands, organizes, and evaluates information using an outline or organizer tool.
- Clarifies main and supporting ideas using evidence, examples, data, and details.
- Connects and compares ideas from various sources and addresses contradictory information.
- Connects information with prior knowledge, evidence, and examples.
- Revises questions or hypothesis as needed.
- Evaluates inquiry process and resources used.
- Discovers relationship among ideas.
- Reviews and reflects how ideas changed with more information.
- Identifies when information does not support tentative thesis.
- Gathers additional information as needed.
- Demonstrates new understanding by drawing relevant conclusions supported by evidence.
- Participates productively in groups to generate information.
- Creates first draft of product.

Before moving to the Express Phase, a student may ask:
- Does my draft or product meet all requirements?
- Have I drawn conclusions that are supported by the evidence?
- Have I organized my information to present it effectively?
- Have I checked for problems and/or gaps?

INQUIRY PHASE: EXPRESS

**Key Dispositions of the
21st-Century Learner:**

- Creativity
- Responsibility
- Mastery
- Self-confidence
- Social Responsibility
  - Leadership and confidence in expressing ideas
    - Presents meaningful grasp of complexity

**At the beginning of the
Express Phase, a student may ask:**

- What type of product or presentation will allow me to present my evidence and conclusions effectively to the intended audience?
- What technology will help me create a product or presentation?
- Have I included everything I need to fulfill the requirements of the assignment?
- Have I practiced enough to be confident in communicating my ideas?

INDICATORS—21st-Century Learner:

- Demonstrates and communicates an authentic, meaningful, and deep understanding of material presented.
- Transforms information to knowledge (meaning and impact).
- Explores diverse presentation formats (i.e., written products, oral and visual presentations, technology products, and/or various combinations).
- Determines appropriate presentation format.
- Creates final product through drafting, reflection, and revision.
- Uses standard citation conventions.
- Rehearses or prepares presentation of product.
- Presents or communicates final product using appropriate format or technology.
- Uses writing process to develop expression of new understandings.

Before moving to the Reflect Phase, a student may ask:

- Have I organized the product or presentation to make my major points and present convincing evidence?
- Did my product or presentation fulfill all the requirements of the assignment?
- Have I practiced enough to be confident in communicating my ideas?

INQUIRY PHASE: REFLECT/ASSESS

Key Dispositions of the
21st-Century Learner:

- Validating accuracy
- Reflection
- Receives criticism and feedback with open mind
- Actively listens
- Testing conclusions
- Questions own views
- Critical stance
- Social responsibility

At the beginning of the
Reflect/Assess Phase, a student may ask:

- Was my product/presentation as effective as I could make it?
- How well did my Inquiry process go?
- What are the questions I need to answer?
- Did I fulfill all the requirements of the assignment?

INDICATORS—21st-Century Learner:

- Develops evaluative criteria.
- Participates in peer evaluation.
- Engages in self-evaluation.
- Asks new questions for continuing Inquiry.

Before moving to another assignment or
personal Inquiry, a student may ask:

- What new understandings did I develop about the topic or idea?
- What did I learn about the Inquiry process?
- What might I do differently next time to improve my Inquiry process or product?
- How can I use the feedback on my final product for my next Inquiry project?

From *Rx for the Common Core: Toolkit for Implementing Inquiry Learning* by Mary Boyd Ratzer and Paige Jaeger. Santa Barbara, CA: Libraries Unlimited. Copyright © 2014.

SOCIAL AND ETHICAL RESPONSIBILITY

Key Dispositions of the 21st-Century Learner:

- Ethical responsibility
- Collaboration
- Respect
- Validating accuracy
- Seeking perspectives
- Initiative
  - Using patterns of evidence to draw conclusions
    - Shows tolerance for perspectives
      - Regulates and assesses behavior
        - Questions own views

At the beginning of this Phase, a student may ask:

- How can I say things in my own words?
- What does academic integrity mean in my school? Is there a policy? What are the consequences of plagiarism?
- Why should we appreciate the opinions of others in a global society?
- Why is it important to cooperate within a group?

INDICATORS—21st-Century Learner:

- Seeks and uses diverse sources and multiple points of view.
- Cites sources accurately and identifies sources of ideas, information, images, and sounds.
- Respects intellectual property rights and seeks permission from a source of ideas, information, images, and sounds where appropriate.
- Respects and acknowledges diverse ideas, perspectives, and backgrounds.
- Contributes to the development and exchange of ideas within the learning community and world.
- Collaborates with others, both in person and through technologies, to design, develop and evaluate information products and solutions.
- Practices safe behaviors in personal and electronic communication and interaction.
- Protects and respects the network of print, electronic, and digital resources.
- Reflects on the product and the process.

Before moving to another assignment or personal Inquiry, a student may ask:

- Is this my own work?
- Is this my creation?
- Did I get appropriate permissions for information, sounds, and images I used?
- Did I cite my sources?

LITERATURE and LITERACY
Engaged Reading

Key Dispositions of the 21st-Century Learner:

- Self-direction
- Curiosity
- Reading skills
- Projects self into another's experience
- Sustained intellectual activity
- Reflection
- Flexibility
- Initiative

At the beginning of Engaged Reading, a student may ask:

- Where do I find choices of reading and / or viewing resources that will match my interests?

- How do I find out about books and films I will enjoy?

INDICATORS—21st-Century Learner:

- Will seek information related to personal interest and pleasure.

- Selects literature based on personal needs, interests, and reading level from a variety of genres.

- Identifies and differentiates between fiction and nonfiction.

- Uses technology to find information in a variety of formats related to personal interests and social interaction.

- Explores award winning works of literature and note worthy authors, illustrators, and producers.

Before moving to another assignment or personal Inquiry, a student may ask:

- Have I read and reflected on books and other media?

- Was I able to locate and reflect on literature and other media that suits my personal interests?

- Did I become familiar with authors?

Literary Response, Critical Analysis, and Evaluation

Key Dispositions of the
21st-Century Learner:

- Critical thinking
- Self-directed
- Reflective
- Curiosity
- Using patterns of evidence to draw conclusions
- Openness to new ideas
- Questioning
- Extends investigation
- Looks for alternate points of view
- Validates accuracy
- Persistence

At the beginning of the Critical Analysis and Evaluation Phase, a student may ask:

- Am I able to critically analyze the material?
- What elements of the text or other media will help me understand?
- What is the connection between literature and the world?

INDICATORS—21st-Century Learner:

- Seeks information related to various dimensions of personal well being, such as career interests, community involvement, health matters, and recreational pursuits.
- Explores a variety of media for reading, listening, and viewing purposes.
- Recognizes author's purpose: persuade, inform, or entertain.
- Uses inferences and deduction to understand.
- Identifies elements of fiction (character, plot, setting, style, theme, point of view) to their personal reading.
- Recognizes characteristics of genres.
- Compares and Contrasts literature published in different medias.
- Thinks and speaks critically about literature.
- Utilizes elements of nonfiction (table of contents, index, boldfaced type, glossary, captions, time lines, diagrams, and keywords).
- Identifies parts of a book (cover, dust jacket, spine, title page, copy right date, end pages, spine label).
- Differentiates between fact and opinion.

Before moving to another assignment or personal Inquiry, a student may ask:

- Did I understand the author's meaning?
- Do I understand the connection between literature and the world?
- Do I have an awareness of the elements of literature?
- Was I able to critically analyze the literature?

From *Rx for the Common Core: Toolkit for Implementing Inquiry Learning* by Mary Boyd Ratzer and Paige Jaeger. Santa Barbara, CA: Libraries Unlimited. Copyright © 2014.

ACKNOWLEDGMENTS

This document was created to embrace the national paradigm shift in educating the 21st-century learner. Its purpose is to provide librarians and teachers with a research and learning model that embraces a collaborative approach to questioning, investigating, problem solving, creating, and contributing.

This research model is based on the "Stripling Inquiry" model that has proven successful around America. We would like to thank the librarians of New York State, as well as ISTE, National Educational Technology Standards for Students and the AASL Dispositions and Responsibilities for 21st-century learners that helped us to shape this document and transform our approach to research and instruction for the 21st-century student.

From *Rx for the Common Core: Toolkit for Implementing Inquiry Learning* by Mary Boyd Ratzer and Paige Jaeger. Santa Barbara, CA: Libraries Unlimited. Copyright © 2014.

The following Inquiry Planners can be used as black line master tools to help consider all the elements of an "Inquiry lesson." Or, these can be used to consider all the elements of Inquiry while planning the Common Core lesson or unit.

Use them. Share them.

Pieces of the Puzzle: *Inquiry, Information, Technology and Common Core Alignment*

The Common Core asks us to create lessons that:
are data driven
are aligned with **college and career expectations**
include **rigorous** content and foster higher-level thought
are built upon standards and **shifts**
are infuse **Information** and imbed **technology** to foster higher-level thought

What do you want your students to know or be able to do, at the end?		Ideas for technology, information integration, and other notes
Content List CCSS strand + Science or SS topic	Begin with the end in mind.	
Students will know, or be able to do What is the enduring understanding you want your students to understand at the end of the unit?		
What can the EQ be? **How can I make this relevant?**		
What is the Big Idea? What is the umbrella question? What is the Moral of the story? What question can I ask to compel students to research, think, and synthesize?		Preassess the EQ with: KWL, Graffiti walls, mind-maps, clickers, Stixy, and more
What will our knowledge product be?		
"Research to build and present knowledge"	How can the student share his knowledge?—Some choices listed →	What technology can we use: * Infographic * Museum box * eTimeline * Prezi. PPT, or alternative * Moviemaker * Animoto * Blabberize * Crazytalk * essay, report * Public Service announcement

(Continued)

How can I preassess?		
Either formal or innovative. How can I capture the baseline knowledge level prior to teaching this to prove my effectiveness and target instruction correctly?		Technology tools? Clickers, Stixy .com, Todaysmeet .com Mind-mapping (vacant?), Graffiti walls, List for me. . . . Pre-test
How will I address the shifts?		
Vocabulary of the discipline **Cool Words that will make you sound smart** (Consider word walls, bookmarks of terms, and more—these should be in post assessment rubrics, tests, etc.		*List the words* you want your students to use knowingly in a "knowledge product." i.e., terminology, core content vocabulary, words they will come across in research
Do I need complex Text? What can they read?	What activity can I link to rich text, after close reading for deeper understanding? Do we need to find a "rich-text" article to embrace close-focused reading?	Lexile.com, ATOS, DRP Library catalog, Word Readability Statistics Books, database articles, primary source documents, ELA novels
Have you raised rigor?		
K–1 N/A 2–3 450–790 4–5 770–980 6–8 955–1,155 9–10 1,080–1,305 11–12 1,215–1,355	List the complexity levels.	• Rigorous? • 50%–50%, fiction and nonfiction • Staircase of Complexity • Reading across the disciplines
What are my TDQs? TDBs		Inquiry? Close reading and response

(Continued)

From *Rx for the Common Core: Toolkit for Implementing Inquiry Learning* by Mary Boyd Ratzer and Paige Jaeger. Santa Barbara, CA: Libraries Unlimited. Copyright © 2014.

Build the Learning Plan: How can I make this student centered?			
What CCSS pedagogy "verbs" are you embracing?	**CCSS language:** Research, draw, evidence, conclude, examine, analyze, solve a problem, understand argue, debate, persuade, critique, support, comprehend, persuade	**Bloom's:** Rote & recall vs. challenge, remembering vs. understanding, analysis, synthesis, applying, analyzing, evaluating, creating	**Inquiry Verbs:** Wonder—focus, investigate, analyze, synthesis, explain, present
Formative Assessment tools:			Clickers, Checklists, discussion rubrics, vocabulary usage, quizzes, questioning, timeline benchmarks, mind-mapping, journaling, tickets to leave, Checking blogs
Hook How can we activate thinking? Link the unknown to something known (Transfer). Video, pictures, brainstorming questions			Video clips, mystery, experiments, KWL, story, etc photos, internet tour, brainstorming
Inquiry, Collaboration, Information, and technology:			
Wonder			Graffiti walls Stixy.com Video clip Picture w/debate Carousel Graffiti placemats KWL
Investigate			Research Collect Data Databases Wikis Blogs (Edmodo-Blackboard) Interview Research to build knowledge

(Continued)

From *Rx for the Common Core: Toolkit for Implementing Inquiry Learning* by Mary Boyd Ratzer and Paige Jaeger. Santa Barbara, CA: Libraries Unlimited. Copyright © 2014.

Synthesize		Draw Conclusions Excel Research to present knowledge Using technology, interact and collaborate
Express Knowledge product—Tech Tool, essay, summative assessment ideas		PPT, Infographic iMovie—MovieMaker Microsoft Word Photobabble Blabberize—Crazytalk Debate Public Service Announcement, Journals, Blogs, reports, etc.
Information Resources Available	See your librarian if you are unsure. Rigor is not Google. CARS = Credible, reliable, accurate, supported info CUB = Current, Utility, and Bias check	Databases Information literacy terms? Digitalvaults.org Exploratorium.edu Gather relevant info conduct research projects Use advanced searches effectively

Bibliography

Alberta Learning, Learning and Teaching Resources Branch. *Focus on Inquiry, A Teacher's Guide to Implementing Inquiry-Based Learning*. Alberta, Canada: Alberta Learning, 2004. Print.

Alstaedter, Laura Levi, and Brett Jones. "Motivating Students' Foreign Language and Culture Acquisition through Web-Based Inquiry." *Foreign Language Annals* 42.4 (2009): 640–657. Print.

Avery, Patricia. "Authentic Student Performance, Assessment Tasks and Instruction." *Authentic Pedagogy* 8.1 (2000): 1–7. Web.

Ballard, Susan. "Developing the Vision: Enhancing Your Professional Practice." *Knowledge Quest* 38.3 (2010): 76–77. Print.

Ballard, Susan. "Opportunity Knocks or the Wolf Is at the Door: ICT Standards and the Common Core." *Teacher Librarian* 38.2 (2010): 69–71. Print.

Barack, Lauren. "Full-Time Librarians Linked to Higher Student Reading Scores." *School Library Journal* (March 6, 2012). Web.

Barron, Brigid, and Linda Darling-Hammond. *"Teaching for Meaningful Learning:* A Review of Research on Inquiry-Based and Cooperative Learning." Stanford University. Edutopia (2008). Web.

Barton, Holly. "Information Literacy: Learning How to Learn." Teachers in Technology Initiative. Rhode Island Foundation. University of Rhode Island (2006). Web.

Bastock, Michelle, et al. "Inquiry Transforms Learning Environments for Students." *Alberta Teachers Association Magazine* 87.2 (2007):1–3. Web.

Black, Susan. "Teachers CAN Engage Disengaged Students." *Education Digest* 69.7 (2004): 39–45. Web.

Board on Testing and Assessment. "Report Brief." Rev. of Education for Life and Work Developing Transferable Knowledge and Skills in the 21st Century, by National Research Council. *National Academies* (2013). Web.

Bryk, Anthony, Jenny K. Nagaoka, and Fred M. Newmann. "Chicago Classroom Demands for Authentic Intellectual Work: Trends from 1997–1999." Consortium on Chicago School Research. Chicago Annenberg Research Project (October 2000). Web.

Butrymozicz, Sarah. "Why are Other Countries Doing Better in Sciences Than the U.S.?" *Hechinger Report* (January 26, 2011). Web.

Callsion, Daniel. "Instructional Trends from AASL Journals: 1972–2007 Part 1: From Teacher-Centered to Student Centered." *School Library Media Activities Monthly* 25.8 (2009): 22–26. Print.

Callison, Daniel, and Leslie Preddy. *The Blue Book on Information Age Inquiry, Instruction and Literacy*. Westport, CT: Libraries Unlimited, 2006.

Cheong, Wendy. "The Power of Questioning." *Connect* 13.4 (2000). Web.

Clark, Richard E. "Putting Students on the Path to Learn." *American Educator* 36.2 (2012): 6–11. Print.

Clyde, Jean Anne, and Angela Hicks. "Immersed in Inquiry." *Educational Leadership* 65 (Summer 2008). Web.

Coatney, Sharon. "Standards for the 21st-Century Learner in Action." *School Library Media Activities Monthly* 25.8 (2009): 27–29. Print.

Conley, David. "Building on the Common Core." *Educational Leadership* 68.6 (2011): 16–21. Print.

Crow, Sherry R. "Information Literacy: What's Motivation Got to Do with It?" *Knowledge Quest* 35.4 (2007): 48–52. Print.

Darling-Hammond, Linda, et al. *Powerful Learning: What We Know About Teaching for Understanding.* San Francisco, CA: John Wiley & Sons Inc., 2008. Print.

Darling-Hammond, Linda, and Frank Adamson "Beyond Basic Skills: the Role of Performance Assessment in Achieving 21st Century Standards of Learning." Stanford Center for Opportunity Policy in Education (2010). Web.

Davies-Hoffman, Kim, and Michelle Costello. "Pedagogy for Librarians: LILAC as a Temporary Measure to Satisfy Library Instructors' Needs." *The NYLA Bulletin* (Fall 2010): 11–12. Print.

"Designing Effective Projects: Project-Based Units to Engage Students." Intel Education. Intel. Web.

Diaz, Shelley, and Sarah Bayliss. "SLJ Summit 2012: Full-Time School Librarians Boost Student Test Scores in Reading, Writing, Says PA Report." *School Library Journal* 58:10 (2012). Web.

Donham, Jean. "Assignments Worth Doing." *School Library Monthly* 28.2 (2011): 5–7. Print.

Farrington, Camille, et al. "Teaching Adolescents to Become Learners: The Role of Noncognitive Factors in Shaping School Performance." *Literature Review.* University of Chicago Consortium on Chicago School Research (June 2012). Web.

Fontichiaro, Kristin. "Nudging Toward Inquiry: Common Core Standards." *School Library Monthly* 28.1 (2011). Web.

Gardner, Howard. "The Five Minds of the Future: Cultivating and Integrating New Ways of Thinking to Empower the Education Enterprise." *The School Administrator* 66.2 (2009). Web.

Gewertz, Catherine. "Common-Core Writers Craft Curriculum Criteria." *Edweek* (July 22, 2011). Web.

Gordon, C.A. "Raising Active Voices in School Libraries: Authentic Learning, Information processing and Guided Inquiry." *SCAN* 28.3 (2009). Web.

Gore, J., et al. *Productive Pedagogy as a Framework for Teacher Education: Towards Better Teaching.* Newcastle: Faculty of Education, University of Newcastle. 2001. Web.

Gourley, Beth. "Inquiry: The Road Less Traveled." *Knowledge Quest* 37.1 (2008): 17–29. Print.

Guccione, Lindsey. "In a World Full of Mandates, Making Spaces for Inquiry." *Reading Teacher* 64.7 (2011): 515–519. Print.

Gutierrez, K., et al. *Connected Learning: an Agenda for Research and Design.* Washington, DC: Foundation Center. 2013. Web.

Harada, Violet. "Empowered Learning: Fostering Thinking Across the Curriculum." Department of Information and Computer Sciences. University of Hawaii (2003). Web.

Harada, Violet, and Joan Yoshina. "Moving from Rote to Inquiry: Creating Learning that Counts." *Library Media Connection* 23.2 (2004): 22–24. Print.

Huxley, Aldous. *Brave new world,.* New York: Harper & Bros., 1946. Print.

"IASL Overview of Alberta. Research Based Shift to Focus on Inquiry." Web.

"The Impact of Library Media Specialists on Students and How It Is Valued by Administrators and Teachers: Findings from the Latest Studies in Colorado and Idaho." *Tech Trends* (July 2011). Web.

"The Impact of New York's School Libraries on Student Achievement and Motivation: Phase I." American Association of School Librarians. American Library Association (2012). Web.

Jaeger, Paige. "Out of the Mud and Onto the Highway: Entrance Ramps for the 21st Century Librarian." *Library Media Connection* 29:5 (2011): 50.

Jaeger, Paige. "Transliteracy—New Library Lingo and What It Means for Instruction." *Library Media Connection* 30:2 (2011): 44–47. Print.

Jaeger, Paige. "Complex Text, Reading and Rigor: Using technology to support the dramatic changes in the CCSS." *Library Media Connection* 30:5 (2012): 30–33.

Jaeger, Paige. "Common Core: Rx for Change." *School Library Monthly* 28:7 (2012): 5–7.

Jaeger, Paige. "Is a Picture Worth $2500.00? Understanding Facts Visually." *School Library Journal* 58:8 (2012): 17.

Jaeger, Paige. "A Match Well Made: the Standards' Emphasis on Information Aligns with Librarians' Skills." *School Library Journal* 58:11(2012): 20.

Jaeger, Paige. "Readability and Reading Fluency." *School Library Journal* 59:3 (2013): 20. Print.

Jaeger, Paige. "Missing in the Common Core." *Library Media Connection* 31:5 (2013).

Jakes, David, et al. "Using the Internet to Promote Inquiry-Based Learning." Internet Innovations, Inc. (March 23, 2002). Web.

Johnson, Doug. "Right Brain Skills and the Media Center: A Whole New Mind(set)." *Knowledge Quest Web Edition* 34.4 (2007). Web.

Jones, Makeba, and Susan Yonezawa. "Student-Driven Research." *Educational Leadership* 66.4 (2009): 65–69. Print.

Kachel, Debra, and Keith Curry Lance. "Latest Study: A Full-time School Librarian Makes a Critical Difference in Boosting Student Achievement." *School Library Journal* 59:3 (2013). Web.

Keeling, Mary. "A District's Journey to Inquiry." *Knowledge Quest* 38.2 (2009): 31–37. Print.

Kohn, Alfie. "It's Not What We Teach; It's What They Learn." *Education Week* (September 10, 2008). Web.

Krajcik, Joseph, Phyllis Blumenfeld, Ron Marx, and Elliot Soloway. "Instructional, Curricular, and Technological Supports for Inquiry in Science Classrooms." In *Inquiry Into Inquiry: Science Learning and Teaching*, ed. Jim Minstrell and Emily H. Van Zee. Washington, DC: American Association for the Advancement of Science Press, 2000. 283–315. Print.

Krashen, S. D. *The Power of Reading: Insights from the Research*, 2nd ed. Westport, CT: Libraries Unlimited, 2004. Print.

Kuhlthau, C. C. "Developing a Model of the Library Search Process: Cognitive and Affective Aspects." *Reference Quarterly* 28.2 (Winter 1988): 232–242. Print.

Kuhlthau, C. C. *Seeking Meaning: A Process Approach to Library and Information Services*. 2nd ed. Westport, CT: Libraries Unlimited. 2004. Print.

Kuhlthau, C. C., L. K. Maniotes, and A. K. Caspari. *Guided Inquiry: Learning in the 21st Century*. Westport, CT: Libraries Unlimited. 2007. Print.

Lance, Keith Curry. "Change in School Librarian Staffing Linked with Change in CSAP Reading Performance, 2005 to 2011." Library Research Service. Colorado State Library (January 2012). Web.

Langer, Judith A., Elizabeth Close, et al. *Guidelines for Teaching Middle and High School Students to Read and Write Well: Six Features of Effective Instruction*. National Research Center on English Learning & Achievement. University at Albany. May 2000. Web.

Larmer, John, and John Mergendoller. "7 Essentials for Project-Based Learning." *Educational Leadership* (September 2010): 34–37. Print.

Levine, Mel. "The Essential Cognitive Backpack." *Educational Leadership* 64.7 (2007): 16–22. Print.

Loertscher, David, and Elizabeth Marcoux. "The Common Core Standards: Opportunities for Teacher-Librarians to Move to the Center of Teaching and Learning." *Teacher Librarian* 38.2 (2010): 8–14. Print.

Lujan, Heidi, and Stephen DiCarlo. "Too Much Teaching, Not Enough Learning: What's the Solution?" *Advances in Physiology Education* 30:1 (2006). Web.

Maestretti, Danielle. "Information Overload." Utne (July–August 2009): 22–23. Print.

Marinak, B. A., and L. B. Gambrell. "Intrinsic Motivation and Rewards: What Sustains Young Children's Engagement with Text?" *Literacy Research and Instruction* 47.1 (2008): 9–26. Web.

Marzano, Robert. *Classroom Assessment & Grading that Work*. Alexandria, VA: Association for Supervision and Curriculum Development, 2006. Print.

McLeod, Scott. "High School Students Know that Their Learning Isn't Relevant." *Big Think* (January 5, 2012). Web.

McMackin, Mary, and Barbara Siegal. "Integrating Research Projects with Focused Writing Instruction." *Reading Online* 4.7 (2001). Web.

McTighe, Jay, and Ken O'Connor. "Seven Practices for Effective Learning." *Educational Leadership* 63.3 (2005): 10–17. Print.

Metlife Survey of the American Teacher: Challenges for School Leadership. Metlife. February 2013. Web.

Munk, Miriam. "Science Pedagogy, Teacher Attitudes, and Student Success." *Journal of Elementary Science Education* (September 22, 2007). Web.

Murdoch, Kath. "What Makes a Good Inquiry Unit?" *EQ* (March 2004). Web.

National Assessment Governing Board. U.S. Department of Education. "Reading Framework for the 2009 National Assessment of Educational Progress." Washington, DC. 2009, 2010, 2012, 2013. Web.

National Evaluation of High School Transformation. "Rigor, Relevance, and Results: the Quality of Teacher Assignments and Student Work in New and Conventional High Schools." American Institutes for Research (July 2005). Print.

"New Jersey Impact of School Libraries on Student Learning." New Jersey Association of School Libraries (NJASL), Center for International Scholarship in School Libraries (CISSL) (2011). Web.

New York Comprehensive Center. "Informational Brief: Impact of School Libraries on Student Achievement." New York State Education Department. New York State Education Department (October 2011). Web.

"New York State P-12 Common Core Learning Standards for English Language Arts & Literacy." NYSED. Engage NY. Web.

Newmann, Fred M., Anthony S. Bryk, and Jenny K. Nagaoka. "Authentic Intellectual Work and Standardized Tests: Conflict or Coexistence." *Consortium on Chicago School Research* (2001). Print.

Newmann, Fred M., M. Bruce King, and Dana L. Carmichael. *Authentic Instruction and Assessment: Common Standards for Rigor and Relevance in Teaching Academic Subjects.* Iowa Department of Education. 2007. Print.

Nichols, Sharon L., and Berliner, David C. "Why has High Stakes Testing So Easily Slipped into Contemporary American Life?" *The Education Digest* 74.4 (2008): 41–48. Web.

Northwest Evaluation Association (NWEA). For Every Child Multiple Measures, What Parents and Educators Want from Assessments (2012). Web.

"NYS P-12 Common Core Learning Standards." NYSED. Curriculum and Instruction (2011). Web.

Oakes, Jeannie, and Marisa Saunders. "Multiple Pathways: Bringing School to Life." *Education Week* 20 (July 2009). Web.

Ontario Ministry of Education. Report of the Expert Panel on Students at Risk in Ontario—2003. "Think Literacy." Web.

Pappas, Marjorie. "Inquiry and 21st-Century Learning." *School Library Media Activities Monthly* 25.9 (2009): 49–51. Print.

Paul, Annie Murphy. "The Trouble with Homework." *New York Times* (September 10, 2011), Sunday ed. SR6. Web.

Purcell, Kristen, Lee Rainie, et al. "How Teens Do Research in the Digital World." Pew Internet. Pew Internet in American Life Project (November 1, 2012). Web.

Scheurman, Geoffrey, and Fred M. Newmann. "Authentic Intellectual Work in Social Studies: Putting Performance before Pedagogy." *Social Education* (1998): 1–5. Web.

"School Libraries Count! National Longitudinal Survey of School Library Programs." American Association of School Librarians (2011). Web.

"School Libraries and Student Achievement 2013." Library Research Service—Colorado State Library. Web.

"The State of America's Libraries, 2012," American Library Associations (ALA) Young Adult Library Services Organization (YALSA). Web.

St. Jarre, Kevin. "They Knew Calculus When They Left: The Thinking Disconnect between High School and University." *Phi Delta Kappan* 90.2 (2008). Web.

Stiggins, Rick, and Jan Chappuis. "What a Difference a Word Makes." *JSD* 27.1 (2006): 10–14. Print.

Stripling, Barbara. "Learning Centered Libraries: Implications from Research." Library Power Public Education Foundation. *SLMQ* 23.3 (Spring 1995). Web.

Stripling, Barbara K., and Hughes-Hassell, Sandra. *Curriculum Connections through the Library.* Englewood Cliffs, CO: Libraries Unlimited, 2003. Print.

Tierney, John. "AP Classes are a Scam." *Atlantic* (October 13, 2012). Web.

Todd, Ross. "From Information to Knowledge: Charting and Measuring Changes in Students' Knowledge of a Curriculum Topic." *Information Research* 11.4 (2006). Web.

Todd, Ross. *The Knowledge Foundation of Information Literacy.* Rutgers University. Center for International Scholarship in School Libraries (2007). Web.

Todd, Ross, Gordon, C. A., and Lu, Y. L. *One Common Goal: Student Learning, Phase 2.* New Brunswick, NJ: Center for International Scholarship in School Libraries. 2011. Web.

Todd, Ross. *School Libraries and Learning: A Research Journey.* Rutgers University. Center for International Scholarship in School Libraries (2010). Web.

Todd, Ross, Carol Gordon, et al. *Report of Findings and Recommendations of the New Jersey School Library Survey.* Center for International Scholarship in School Libraries. School of Communications and Information. Rutgers State University. New Jersey Association of School Librarians (July 2012). Web.

Toppo, Greg. "Teachers are Key for Students Who Like Learning and Remain Curious." *USA Today* (July 5, 2007). Web.

Trinkle, Catherine. "Library Media Specialist's Word Wall and Beyond: Integrating the Five Components of Reading Instruction." *School Library Media Activities Monthly* 23.1 (2006): 30–43. Print.

"UbD Exchange Helpful WWW Links." Jay McTighe and Associates Educational Consulting. Web.

Wiggins, Grant, and Jay McTighe. *Understanding by Design, Expanded 2nd Edition.* Alexandria, VA: Association for Supervision and Curriculum Development, 2005. Print.

Wilhelm, Jeffrey, and Peggy Jo Wilhelm. "Inquiring Minds Learn to Read, Write, and Think: Reaching All Learners Through Inquiry." *Middle School Journal* (May 2010): 39–46. Print.

Wolk, Steven. "School as Inquiry." *Phi Delta Kappan* 90.2 (2008): 15–122. Web.

Wolk, Steven. "Why Go to School?" *Phi Delta Kappan* 88.9 (2007): 648–659. Web.

Yager, Robert E., AeRan Choi, Stuart O. Yager, and Hakan Akcay. "Comparing Science Learning Among 4th-, 5th-, and 6th-Grade Students: STS Versus Textbook-Based Instruction." *Journal of Elementary Science Education* 21.2 (2009): 15–24. Print.

Zimmerman, B.J. "Self-efficacy: An Essential Motive to Learn." *Contemporary Educational Psychology* 25 (2000): 82–91. Print.

Zmuda, Allison. "Springing into Active Learning." *Educational Leadership* 66.3 (2008): 38–42. Print.

Zmuda, Allison. "What Does it Really Look Like When Students are Learning in the Library Media Center?" *School Library Media Activities Monthly* 25.1 (2008): 25–27. Print.

Index

About the Authors

PAIGE JAEGER, MLIS, is a library administrator serving 84 school libraries in up-state New York. She delivers professional development at the local, state, and national levels and is currently serving on the American Association School of Librarians (AASL) Task Force for the Common Core. Jaeger has been a frequent contributor to national library journals such as *School Library Journal, School Library Monthly,* and *Library Media Connection.*

MARY BOYD RATZER, now retired, is a 37-year veteran teacher and school librarian at the Shenendehowa Central Schools, Clifton Park, New York. Serving as adjunct faculty, she taught curriculum and supervised internships in the school media track at the University at Albany, the State University of New York from 1987 to 2007. Actively engaged as a professional development consultant for the past 10 years, she has fostered Inquiry-based learning and real-world strategies for the Common Core. A frequent resource for the New York State Department of Education since 1995, Ratzer has contributed directly to curricular, assessment, and standards reform.